# WHOLE PLANTS COOKBOOK

# WHOLE PLANTS COOKBOOK

Based on the research of T. Colin Campbell
as presented in *The China Study* (2005),
coauthored by T. Colin Campbell, PhD,
& Thomas M. Campbell II, MD

LeAnne Campbell Disla, PhD

Foreword by T. Colin Campbell

Craxy Frog Publishers
*Durham, North Carolina*

*Whole Plants Cookbook. Based on the research*
*of T. Colin Campbell, as presented in* The China Study
*(2005), coauthored by T. Colin Campbell, PhD,*
*and Thomas M. Campbell II, MD*

This book was printed on acid-free, recycled paper.
According to the Environmental Paper Network Paper Calculator
(www.papercalculator.org), using this 30% post-consumer paper
saved about 32 mature trees.

ISBN 978-0-9832509-1-3
Library of Congress Control Number: 2011929328

Craxy Frog Publishers
427 Kingsbury Drive
Durham, North Carolina 27712

# CONTENTS

## ❋ *Breakfast Dishes* ❋

## ❋ *Appetizers and Salads* ❋

# ❋ Soups ❋

# ❋ Sandwiches ❋

# ❋ Entrees ❋

## ❋ *Side Dishes* ❋

## ❈ *Desserts* ❈

*Remember to consume a variety of whole plant foods*

| fruits | grains | leaves | roots | legumes | flowers | nuts | mushrooms |
|--------|--------|--------|-------|---------|---------|------|-----------|

# FOREWORD

I am prejudiced, and I might as well say so up front. The author of this book is my daughter, LeAnne Campbell Disla. But, prejudiced or not, I know her style of cooking, her recipes (I've tried many), her commitment to good nutrition, and her ability, as a very busy professional, to prepare quick, nutritious meals.

In considerable part, LeAnne engaged her family with this book project. Both of her boys were ready and willing, and they have now become good cooks in their own right. Her mother, Karen, and her sister-in-law, Kim, added a few recipes and helped with the taste testing. And I helped too—with the tasting, that is; twice I tasted the recipes that my wife added to this book.

The tasty recipes in this book are consistent with the health message of *The China Study*, which my son, Tom, and I wrote. This book is also written with the intent of helping people prepare quick, nutritious meals after a hard day's work.

One of the features of LeAnne's book is her use of recipes with no added fat, little or no added salt, and her minimal, judicious use of sweetening agents. Her no-added-fat strategy may be questioned by some folks who cannot quite accept the idea of not using oil or fat in their daily diet. The scientific evidence shows that we should try to avoid using *added* fat, especially for those who are either at high risk of getting a degenerative disease (which is most people) or who have already been diagnosed with one (e.g., cardiovascular diseases, cancers, diabetes and other metabolic disorders, and obesity). I am using the term "added" fat in order to distinguish it from whole plant-based foods that are high in fat, because the latter often contain a natural supply of antioxidants, fiber, and the right kind of protein.

I know that for many people who have always eaten the typical American diet, switching to a no-added-fat diet can be challenging—at least at first. But it's important to know that fat has been proven to be addictive, often causing people to consume increasing amounts over time. Eventually, it becomes quite difficult for many people to recover from this addiction. As with any other addiction, some people not only find it difficult to switch; they sometimes become unusually defensive about their preferences.

But change is possible. It only takes time, perhaps as much as a few months for some individuals. And once that change is achieved, we discover new flavors among whole plant-based foods that we hardly knew existed. Once people arrive at this healthier place, many then discover that if, out of curiosity, they switch back to that old dish floating in fat, they experience some difficulties—perhaps even real intestinal disturbances—or they may find that the old stuff tastes more like a good dose of grease. The same is also true when switching to a low-salt diet, although the "addictive" mechanism may be quite different in that case.

I have often been asked—a few hundred times, I think—what do my family and I eat? Although I try to respond on the spot, I know well that my very limited answers cannot be satisfying to those looking to make real lifestyle changes. Now I am happy to say that there is a cookbook that comes about as close to the real deal for our family as I can imagine. This is it.

T. Colin Campbell, PhD
Coauthor of the best-selling *The China Study*
Professor Emeritus of Nutritional Biochemistry
Cornell University

# ACKNOWLEDGMENTS

We went through several steps in putting together this cookbook, one of which involved testing the recipes. Elise Murphy, with support from the TCC Foundation, organized the initial testing process. There were many wonderful people who assisted with testing, including Dan and Becky Mikles, Nancy Porteous, Julia Sokol, Kathy Pollard, Dawn Shepard, Ann Parkin, Patricia Hale, Louann Savage, and Richard Revell. Later the recipes were retested, and I would like to thank my mother, Karen Campbell, who helped with this process. Once the recipes were perfected, we prepared the different dishes so we could take pictures of them. I would like to thank Steven Disla, my son, for taking the photographs—sometimes more than 150 pictures for each recipe. I would also like to thank those who assisted in preparing the recipes to be photographed: my mother, Karen Campbell, once again; my sons, Steven and Nelson Disla; and their close friends, Katie Tolley and Nikolai Beer. They spent countless hours helping make this book a reality. As Steven said, "God, why do I always smell like onions?"

I would also like to thank those who contributed their own recipes to this cookbook. In particular, I want to thank my sister-in-law, Kimberly Campbell, who has been preparing plant-based meals for more than twenty years. I would also like to thank my mother for contributing her recipes to this cookbook. As we all know, she is AMAZING.

And finally, I would like to thank all the people who provided moral support for this project. Friends, such as Meredith Condor and Beth Silberman, always provided a vote of confidence and encouragement. My family—especially my parents, Karen and Colin Campbell, and my sons, Steven and Nelson Disla—were instrumental in this entire process. Without them, this book would never have happened. Their continual support and encouragement made the whole book possible. And Dad, thanks for always pushing me to stay on track, even when I had other things to do. You guys are the BEST!

# INTRODUCTION

## MY JOURNEY TOWARD A PLANT-BASED DIET

What one eats is a personal choice, often based on what each individual finds tasty, satisfying, familiar, or readily available. When people ask me to think about what I eat and why I eat what I do, I have to pause for a minute. My own life experiences and the experiences of the individuals closest to me—most notably those who cared for me as a child—have affected me, just as such experiences affect everyone. When I was a child, it was often my mother who chose the food I was to eat, simply because she cooked and prepared all of our family's meals. We ate these meals with gusto: pork chops, mashed potatoes, green beans, spaghetti with meatballs, or a large plate of fried chicken. These dinners were topped off with homemade desserts and ice cream.

It wasn't until my junior year in high school that my diet began to change. My father, Dr. T. Colin Campbell, was conducting his research, later detailed in *The China Study*, currently an international best seller. Based on his research, he suggested to my mother that we start following a diet centered more on plant-based foods than on animal-based foods. As a family, we slowly began transitioning toward a plant-based diet. Instead of serving meat as the main menu item, my mother began to use meat more sparingly, as a side dish or only for added flavor. We changed from eating a large slab of ham with a side of macaroni to having one or two slices of ham cut into small chunks and added to a large casserole dish of scalloped potatoes, serving eight people.

My mother was always an amazing cook; while I was growing up, I loved her cooking. So when I went away to college, I sought out the familiar, comforting foods of my childhood, which often included animal products. Until this point, my food choices had been based solely on my cravings and what I found to be tasty. My college friends and I would order that late-night pizza with extra cheese and sausage, followed by a large ice cream sundae smothered in hot fudge sauce. It really wasn't until I graduated from college that I truly began to question why I was eating what I was eating.

In trying to pinpoint the exact experiences that led to my transition to a plant-based diet, I can remember a couple of distinct and slightly more encompassing memories. Upon graduation, I was accepted into the Peace Corps. For the first time, I would really be on my own. This was the late 1980s, and cell phones were not common, making communication from remote areas difficult. In fact, I was stationed in one of the more rural areas of the Dominican Republic, working directly with impoverished families and their malnourished children. There was one family in particular—and specifically one child—that I became attached to. Anita was fourteen months old and weighed barely nine pounds. Her grandmother cared for her while her mother was in the city looking for employment. Anita's grandmother often passed by the clinic where I lived and worked.

One day it had been raining, and the grandmother was carrying a few sacks of food that she had bought in town. She had also taken Anita—who had developed a bronchial infection—to the doctor. I could see Anita's grandmother struggling to carry both the food and the child, so I offered to carry Anita. As we walked the two miles up the mountain back to Anita's home, I could feel her little heartbeat, so close to my chest. At times she was so still. I had to stop and put my ear down close to her face to hear if she was still breathing.

That evening when I returned to the clinic, I stayed in my room. Usually I would have gone to my neighbor's house to play dominoes or just hang out in their kitchen to share stories. But that evening I wanted to be by myself. Earlier that week, I had started reading the book *Diet for a Small Planet* by Frances Moore Lappé—a book that really resonated with me that evening. As I had taken Anita up the mountain, I passed a thousand-acre cattle farm, as I usually did. The owners of this farm lived abroad, and when they returned to the D.R., they stayed in their second home in a high-class tourist area. Those living around the farm never saw any benefits from their large, well-off neighbor. The meat from the cattle was used only to feed a small portion of the local population—those who could afford it. But those who needed it most received nothing. The comforts on the farm far exceeded the conditions within the homes surrounding it. The cattle had ample land to graze on; Anita, her family, and several of their neighbors lived in small, cramped quarters. Large bins of water with proper plumbing and faucets were readily available for the cattle at any time, allowing them an abundant supply of water. Anita's family and their neighbors did not have this same luxury. To obtain water they had to walk a long way to the river and then carry it back to their homes in gallon jugs—and even then, the water was often contaminated.

This struck me as being grossly unfair. Looking at this paradox from a humanitarian perspective, I began to question the production of beef. I thought that perhaps I could take one step toward reducing my consumption of animal-based foods so resources could be used more efficiently.

There was another experience during my time in the Peace Corps that made an impact on my dietary choices, this time from more of an animal-rights perspective. Near the end of my Peace Corps tour I was stationed farther up the mountain, and I was in the process of building a school. Traveling from the worksite to the small house where I stayed involved crossing a rather large river, which was relatively easy to do on my motorcycle.

In the field beside my house, there was a small pasture where a goat lived. This goat seemed to be rather curious and attentive to what I was doing. He often came to the fence to follow me around the yard. I started feeding him some of my kitchen scraps, undoubtedly making him even more attentive. He was the first thing I saw each morning when I went outside, and a neighbor claimed that when I returned from work, he would hear my motorcycle, come running to the side of the fence next to my yard, and wait for me as I pushed my motorcycle to the back of the house. I became attached to the goat, who patiently waited for me each day, morning and evening.

One day I came home and saw something that really disturbed me. As I pushed my motorcycle up the back yard, I looked toward the pasture for the goat. There he was— dangling from the fence. His throat had been cut, and his blood was splattered across my yard. His eyes seemed to be following me as I pushed my motorcycle up the path. Those eyes were no longer smiling; they were pleading, in deep pain, almost begging me to help. But I could not do anything. His blood continued to flow slowly down my yard. I felt sick. I turned and went inside.

That evening my neighbors brought me a plate of goat meat, telling me it was well seasoned. I could not eat it. I could not help but see his pleading eyes. This was when I stopped eating meat altogether.

I returned home from the Peace Corps with my own beliefs, from both a humanitarian perspective and an animal-rights perspective. At this time, my father was conducting his own research. And everything he was finding suggested that from a health perspective, eliminating animal-based foods and eating a whole foods, plant-based diet was absolutely essential. As stated in *The China Study* (p. 348):

> *Never before has there been such a mountain of empirical research supporting a whole foods, plant-based diet.* Now, for example, we can obtain images of the arteries in the heart, and then show conclusively, as Drs. Dean Ornish and Caldwell Esselstyn Jr. have done, that a whole-foods, plant-based diet reverses heart disease. We now have the knowledge to understand how this actually works. Animal protein, even more than saturated fat and dietary cholesterol, raises blood cholesterol levels in experimental animals, individual humans, and entire populations. International comparisons between countries show that populations subsisting on traditional plant-based diets have far less heart disease, and studies of individuals within single populations show that those who eat more plant-based foods not only have lower cholesterol levels but also less heart disease. *We now have a deep and broad range of evidence showing that a whole foods, plant-based diet is best for the heart.*
>
> Never before have we had such a depth of understanding of how diet affects cancer

both on a cellular level as well as a population level. Published data show that animal protein promotes the growth of tumors. Animal protein increases the levels of a hormone, IGF-1, which is a risk factor for cancer, and high-casein (the main protein of cow's milk) diets allow more carcinogens into cells, which allow more dangerous carcinogen products to bind to DNA, which allow more mutagenic reactions that give rise to cancer cells, which allow more rapid growth of tumors once they are initially formed. Data show that a diet based on animal-based foods increases females' production of reproductive hormones over their lifetime, which may lead to breast cancer. *We now have a deep and broad range of evidence showing that a whole foods, plant-based diet is best for cancer.*

Never before have we had technology to measure the biomarkers associated with diabetes, and the evidence to show that blood sugar, blood cholesterol, and insulin levels improve more with a whole foods, plant-based diet than with any other treatment. Intervention studies show that when people who have type 2 diabetes are treated with a whole foods, plant-based diet, they may reverse their disease and go off their medications. A broad range of international studies shows that type 1 diabetes, a serious autoimmune disease, is related to cow's milk consumption and premature weaning. We now know how our autoimmune system can attack our own bodies through a process of molecular mimicry induced by animal proteins that find their way into our bloodstream. We also have tantalizing evidence linking multiple sclerosis with animal food consumption and especially dairy consumption. Dietary intervention studies have shown that diet can help slow, and perhaps even halt, multiple sclerosis. *We now have a deep and broad range of evidence showing that a whole foods, plant-based diet is best for diabetes and autoimmune diseases.*

Never before have we had such a broad range of evidence showing that diets containing excess animal protein can destroy our kidneys. Kidney stones arise because the consumption of animal protein creates excessive calcium and oxalate in the kidney. We know now that cataracts and age-related macular degeneration can be prevented by foods containing large amounts of antioxidants. In addition, research has shown that cognitive dysfunction, vascular dementia caused by small strokes, and Alzheimer's are all related to the food we eat. Investigations of human populations show that our risk of hip fracture and osteoporosis is made worse by diets high in animal-based foods. Animal protein leaches calcium from the bones by creating an acidic environment in the blood. *We now have a deep and broad range of evidence showing that a whole foods, plant-based diet is best for our kidneys, bones, eyes, and brains.*

More research can and should be done, but the idea that whole foods, plant-based diets can protect against and even treat a wide variety of chronic diseases can no longer be denied. No longer are there just a few people making claims about a plant-based diet based on their personal experience, philosophy, or the occasional supporting scientific study. Now there are hundreds of detailed, comprehensive, well-done research studies that point in the same direction.

Armed with his work and my own personal beliefs and experiences, I began consuming a diet that was close to being completely plant-based: no animal, meat, or dairy products. I now have two sons who have been raised on a diet that is close to 100 percent plant-based. At the time of this writing, they are sixteen and seventeen years old. As my mother did for me, I have tried to use food not only to nourish them but also to create tasty and healthy dishes.

### RAISING CHILDREN TO CONSUME A PLANT-BASED DIET

I am often asked about raising children who consume a strict plant-based diet. Here are some answers to the more common questions:

*Do children who are raised on a plant-based diet lack nutrients?*
*How does this diet affect their physical and mental growth?*

Based on the experiences I have had with my sons, I see no evidence that being raised on a plant-based diet has stunted or damaged their physical or mental growth. In fact, it has been quite the opposite. Steven, who is seventeen years old, and Nelson, who is sixteen, are both in excellent physical condition and have always been incredibly active and exceptional athletes, both playing on sports teams since the ages of four and five. Steven is 6'3" and Nelson is a little over 5'10"; both boys are muscular and well-toned. Since entering school, they have consistently earned close to all As and have been very alert and quick-witted. Both have won countless academic and athletic awards. Furthermore, they have rarely been sick. So I would say a plant-based diet has not harmed them in the least. Instead, it has nourished their mental and physical potentials.

*Where do they get their protein and calcium from if they don't drink milk?*
*What do they drink?*

When you consume enough calories from whole plant-based foods, plant foods provide all the protein you need. It's been an age-old myth that you cannot get the proper amount of protein from plant-based foods. In place of cow's milk, the boys use rice milk on their cereal; in place of other dairy products in recipes, we often substitute soy milk or rice milk. We also use these same products in plant-based desserts and ice cream. With most meals, instead of drinking a glass of milk, we often drink water. We try to drink at least six to eight glasses of water a day.

*What about when they go to school? How do the other children respond to them?*

In school, the boys take their own lunches from home. Often they bring leftovers from dinner the night before or from earlier in the week. They heat their meals up in the morning, before they go to school, and take them to school in insulated containers. If they don't take leftovers, they make sandwiches, several of which are included in this cookbook, such as Eggless Salad Sandwiches (p. 78), Hummus Wraps (p. 81), Granola Wraps (p. 80), or peanut butter and jelly sandwiches. When their school friends used to make comments about their food, the boys would occasionally make a game of it. My younger son would call it "the mystery mix" and ask his friends to guess what he was eating. The more different and strange his food appeared, the more he would enjoy the game. One of his favorite "mystery mixes" was Dominican Rice and Beans (p. 98), served with Fiesta Potato Salad (p. 55), which has a bright pink tinge from beets.

As is the case with many things in life, it was their attitude toward their dietary preferences, feeling comfortable with who they were and why they ate this way, that made it easy for them. Now that they are older, they no longer engage in this game. Often their classmates ask to taste their food, and their friends—much to their own surprise—often want more.

*What do they do when they go to their friends' homes and are offered meat and/or dairy-based ice cream?*

My son's friends and their families respect their dietary choices and have never forced or bullied them into eating meat or dairy products. In fact, their friends' parents' reactions have usually been the opposite: preparing a meat- and dairy-free meal that everyone at the table would enjoy, usually a pasta dish. However, when my sons travel or go on vacation with their friends' families, I will usually pack food for them to take, often rice milk and additional fruit or snacks, sometimes hummus. Their closest friends are actually very accommodating, stopping at fast-food restaurants where everyone finds food that they can enjoy, such as Subway, where the boys can order a vegetable sub, or a restaurant where they can buy burritos, such as Moe's, Chipotle, or Qdoba. Regardless of the specific restaurant, my sons know what they can order.

However, they have occasionally visited friends who didn't know what to feed them. In these instances, I made sure they ate a meal before going to the friend's house and sometimes packed additional snacks for them to take. It has always worked out, even when we lived in areas of the Deep South, where vegetarianism is rare. During the two years that we lived in a small town in Mississippi, my son's friend's parents were some of the most accommodating people of all.

*How do you get children to eat their vegetables?*

I'm asked this question a lot. I think the answer has to do with the family environment. Children will generally eat the foods that their parents eat. Fortunately for my sons, I love plant-based food, so I have always cooked different dishes with a lot of fresh vegetables, grains, and legumes. This is what they see on a daily basis. For instance, my sons don't like black olives, and I don't use them when I cook because I'm not a fan of olives. My sister-in-law loves black olives; she cooks with them all the time. As toddlers, her children ate them often.

But it's more than what you eat in front of them. It's also important to invite children to help in the kitchen. Have them select a recipe, and if they can, have them prepare the dish too. By being personally involved in preparing meals, children are more motivated to eat what they prepare. As my sons helped with this cookbook and prepared different dishes, they were much more willing to try new food, especially the dishes that they prepared. Dr. Antonia Demas, who has worked extensively in schools across the country, has done research showing that children who prepare their own food are willing to eat their own dishes, even if the dishes contain vegetables that the kids previously disliked. Dr. Demas has created a curriculum called "Food Is Elementary" (available at http://www.foodstudies.org) based on her research. The fact is that kids who cook take pride in the food they prepare and will be more excited to try new things.

THE GARDEN APPROACH:
CHOOSING A WIDE VARIETY OF PLANT FOODS

As you look through the recipes in this cookbook, you will notice that there are plant symbols denoting which part of the plant is being used in the recipe. One of the interpretations of my father's research was that the consumption of a variety of the different parts of whole plants promotes optimal health. Grains, fruits, leaves, flowers, roots, legumes—almost every part of the plant—are edible, nutritious, and delicious. Each part has a different nutrient composition. Here are some examples:

> LEGUMES are a good source of protein, fiber, and iron.
> GRAINS are rich in carbohydrates, fiber, minerals, and B vitamins.
> LEAVES are rich in antioxidant vitamins, fiber, and complex carbohydrates.
> ROOTS have lots of carbohydrates, and some even have carotenoids.

Thus, it's important to consume a variety of plants so that you obtain a full complement of nutrients. Each recipe contains plant icons to show what part of the plant you are consuming and to encourage you to consume as many different plant parts at a given meal, on a given day, and across a week or month.

Knowing how these nutrients behave in the plant helps us understand how they are used in the human body as well. For instance, roots, seeds, and tree nuts store energy and are generally higher in fat and carbohydrates. They are critical components in starting the next generation of plants, especially in generating plant growth when the weather becomes favorable. If fat is a plant's predominant form of energy storage, as is the case for beans, peas, and tree nuts, that plant will also need to include substances that help prevent the fat from spoiling and becoming rancid through oxidation. The solution to this is antioxidants, such as vitamins and some minerals (e.g., vitamin E and selenium).

Some plants store carbohydrates as a source of energy for their offspring, such as the starch in cereal grains and tubers. These energy-storing foods provide their energy to us as well. In a plant-based diet, about 80% of our total energy consumption comes from foods that store most of their energy as carbohydrates and fat. When these energy-

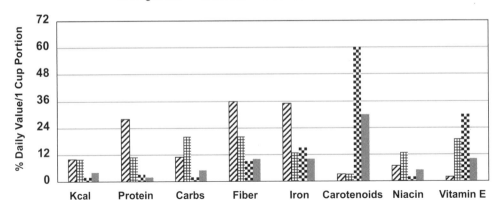

containing foods are growing in an environment where they need to be protected from the elements, while waiting for new plant growth they use tough fibers to create a shell-like outer coat, such as the bran layer of grains (this is what we mean by "whole" grains: grains that are milled without first removing the bran). Most plants use fiber to create a rigid structure to keep them erect. We humans use these fibers, many of which we do not digest, to effectively carry our food through our intestinal tracts—a very normal and healthy process.

Because plants use the carbon atom (1) to create the basic chemical structure of organic molecules (fats, carbohydrates, proteins, and vitamins) and (2) to transport energy during its metabolism in our bodies, carbon needs to be "fixed" in the plants. Plants capture carbon dioxide from the air during photosynthesis; the carbon dioxide is then loaded up with energy from sunlight to form carbohydrates. When we humans consume these plants, we oxidize their carbohydrates to release energy for our own use. Photosynthesis, which takes place in the colored part of the plant that is rich in chlorophyll, involves a sensitive energy transfer process that is capable of leaking highly oxidizing chemicals called radicals, which could damage nearby plant tissue. Plants control this potential damage by surrounding the photosynthesis region with layers of antioxidants, like the hundreds (perhaps thousands) of carotenoids, such as beta carotene and lycopene. This is why the colored parts of plants—greens, reds, and yellows—contain so many antioxidants. These substances are very useful for preventing cancers and cardiovascular diseases.

Another connection between plant and animal functions concerns the formation and use of protein. This molecule is unique in that it contains nitrogen, a basic atom of the amino acids of protein. Both plants and animals need to consume protein (which is to say, they need nitrogen), and they recycle it as an essential part of nature. As they do with carbon dioxide, plants "fix" nitrogen from the air. Microorganisms living within nodules on the roots of legumes, beans, and peas help to fix the nitrogen into the plants so they can make their protein. These foods, therefore, are rich in protein.

There are many, many other examples demonstrating the dependence of humans on plants and vice versa. Plants gather chemicals from the air, water, and soil to make nutrients that animals (humans) use. Humans break these foods down to extract their nutrients, use them, and then excrete their by-products back into the environment for plants to use. The interdependence of animals, plants, and microorganisms sustains life for all groups. Plants make or gather the nutrients essential for our existence (carbohydrates, proteins, fats, vitamins, minerals). With the exception of vitamin B12, which is made by microorganisms, plants provide all the nutrients that we need, in the right amounts and proportions.

In summary, it is very important to consume a variety of plants to make sure we are getting all the nutrients we need. Thus, this book uses the garden approach for all of its recipes, stressing the need to choose a wide variety of plant foods. For instance, I am trying to stress the need to consume the entire plant. However, we don't often consume an entire plant in a given meal or perhaps in a given day or even a given week. For this reason, I have broken the plant into seven categories—roots, leaves, fruits, grains, legumes, flowers, and nuts—and then I added mushrooms as a separate category because they can't be easily categorized as part of a plant. The intent of this categorization is to make you aware of the different parts of the plant and to help you think about consuming all parts of the plant. This is not meant to be a strict guideline but merely a framework to use in trying to put together a nutrient-balanced meal.

I created these categories rather simply. Obviously, roots are the parts of plants that grow below the ground. Leaves include all lettuces, kale, spinach, celery, collards, swiss chard, cabbage, and so on. Fruits are the parts of plants that contains seeds, such as tomatoes, apples, peppers, cucumbers, pumpkins, and oranges. Grains consist of the seeds themselves: wheat, corn, barley, quinoa, oats, and the like. Legumes are made up of all the different types of beans: soy, pinto, red, black, kidney, and even peanuts. Flowers are broccoli, cauliflower, dandelions, et cetera. For nuts, I'm including all tree nuts. The next step is to put this great variety of plant parts together into a nutritious meal.

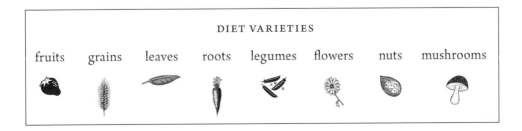

DIET VARIETIES

fruits      grains      leaves      roots      legumes      flowers      nuts      mushrooms

## *Planning*

If you're like me, you probably don't have much time during the week to cook. I often work long hours, and when I come home, I'm exhausted. I want to cook something fast and easy. I've found that a small amount of time invested in menu planning will save time, energy, and money.

In preparing a menu for the week, I try to incorporate a wide range of plant products, including foods from all the different categories of plant parts. Once I have my menu, I make a list of what I need to buy in order to prepare the dishes. I buy only what's on my list. I save shopping time by getting all my ingredients in a single weekly trip. I find that I save money when I use a prepared weekly menu.

You don't have to prepare a complete menu for every meal. Breakfasts are usually the same from day to day, so I simply include some breakfast foods on my shopping list. Lunches are also similar to the previous evening's meal. I generally prepare extra food each evening so we will have leftovers for the following day. When buying lunch food, I make sure to have whole wheat or other whole grain bread or wraps for sandwiches, in case we don't have enough leftovers. Then I buy plenty of fruit for snacks during the day. For dinners, I will prepare a menu with some simple dishes, such as Crock-Pot soups and a couple of dishes that are easy to double. One day during the week is dedicated to leftovers, usually Friday.

*New Century Nutrition* (1996), a newsletter based on the work done in China and coordinated by Dr. Amy Lanou, Bob Conrow, Christy Cox, Susan Neulist, T. Nelson Campbell, and myself, suggested taking the following steps when planning a weekly menu:

- Set aside time to plan a menu for the week.
- Look through your low-fat cookbooks (such as *Whole Plants Cookbook*) for recipe ideas (a mix of familiar favorites with a few new recipes each week usually works best).
- Select three or four main dishes, and plan to prepare enough of each to provide at least two meals (this will provide all your dinners for the week as well as some lunches).
- Make a list of all the ingredients you'll need for these recipes.
- Add some fresh vegetables for salads and side dishes.
- Add foods you'll need for breakfasts and lunches (whole grain breads, whole grain cereals, fresh fruit and vegetables, etc.).
- Add any staples you might need to restock, including spices. It's helpful to keep a running shopping list on the refrigerator or in some other convenient place in the kitchen where these items can be listed as soon as

you use them up, or even better, as soon as you notice that you're getting low.

- Don't go grocery shopping when you're hungry! Have something to eat before going to the store.
- Save your menus and shopping lists. You can reuse them or modify them for future menu planning.

## *Transitioning from a diet high in animal products*

Transitioning from a diet high in animal products to a plant-based diet is a journey. There are certain foods that are made to resemble animal products, and when first transitioning these foods can be used in their place. For instance, tofu dogs (vegan hot dogs) can be used to replace hot dogs, as well as (soy-based) meat crumbles in place of ground beef or vegan (soy-based) chicken and bacon. However, based on the findings of *The China Study*, it is recommended to select whole plant-based foods in their native state, rather than trying to obtain specific nutrients from highly processed foods. This recommendation is based on three important points:

1. Optimal nutrition is based upon eating food rather than nutrient supplements.
2. The closer foods are to their native states—prepared with minimal cooking, salting, and processing—the greater the long-term health benefits will be.
3. Choose locally and/or organically grown produce whenever possible.

The ultimate goal is to move toward a whole foods diet while choosing cooking methods that retain the nutritional value of the food and minimize the addition of fat, salt, and sugar. Let's take a look at the nutritional values of three lunches, ranging from fully processed to minimally processed (see p. 12). The differences in the nutritional breakdown are quite impressive.

## *Careful preparation of food*

My recommendations for food preparation are based on two key suggestions made by *New Century Nutrition*: (1) Choose food that is as close as possible to its native state. (2) Choose cooking methods that retain the nutritional value of the food and minimize the addition of fat, salt, and sugar. I particularly want to focus on the following material, adapted from *New Century Nutrition*'s guidelines for cooking and storage:

Paying attention to how food is stored and prepared can preserve most of the natural health-giving properties of the food. Probably the best way to eat a

| Whole Foods Lunch | Less Processed Lunch | All Processed Lunch |
| --- | --- | --- |
| Rice and corn salad (corn, rice, nuts, veggies with dressing) | Peanut butter and jelly sandwich | Hot dog, bun, catsup |
| Orange/banana | Oatmeal cookies | Potato chips |
| | Orange juice | Twinkie, cola |

COMPARISON OF THE NUTRIENT CONTENT OF THREE LUNCHES

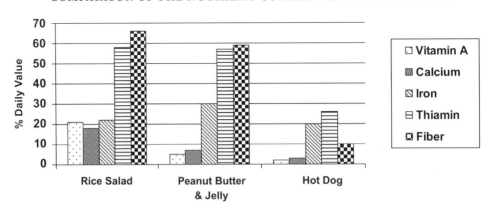

HOW MUCH SALT AND CHOLESTEROL IS IN YOUR LUNCH?

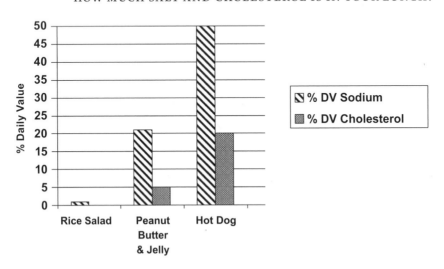

tomato is standing in the garden. Pick the fruit, rub it on your shirt to shine it up and dust it off, and then enjoy every juicy, delicious bite while the sun warms your back. While this is nutritionally (and experientially) ideal, it really is not practical for most people on a regular basis. So the next best thing is to choose storage and preparation methods that maintain as much of this freshness, vitality, and nutritional value as possible.

What can you do to serve your food in its most nutritious state? Several key steps in the journey of food from the farm to the table are important to consider. Storage time and method are both important. Generally, the longer the storage time and the higher the temperature, the greater the loss of nutrients. Storage time includes the time it takes to transport the food from the farm to store, how long it stays in the store, and how long it sits in your home or the restaurant before it is cooked and/or eaten. Especially with fresh produce, the shorter the time between picking and eating, the more nutrients the food retains. Did you know that when asparagus is kept for two days at room temperature, it loses half of its vitamin C? Similarly, corn loses half of its sugar and sweetness in just one day.

### *Storage methods can also affect nutrient retention*

- Chilling produce slows down the degradation reactions that destroy vitamins and sugar.
- Keeping foods such as flour and cereal dry retards bacterial growth.
- Frozen vegetables often have a higher nutrient content than fresh foods that have been kept for a few days. To maintain the nutrients in a frozen food, however, it must be kept well frozen until right before it is used.

Even the freshest, best-stored foods, however, can have their nutrient levels severely decreased by their cooking methods. Losses of vitamin C and some of the B vitamins due to cooking are commonly as high as 65 to 70 percent!

Exposure to water, air, and light as well as heat can decrease nutrient levels in some foods. For example, riboflavin (one of the B vitamins) is sensitive to light, so foods rich in this nutrient should be kept in the dark as much as possible. Antioxidants like vitamin C and beta carotene can be destroyed by exposure to the oxygen in air, so it's important to keep fruit and root vegetables uncut so that the skins protect them or in airtight containers until you use them.

Water-soluble vitamins—vitamins B and C—from cut greens, stems, and roots are readily leached into cooking water; therefore, steaming or microwaving are often preferred cooking methods. If you use the cooking liquid in the dish or save it for later use in a soup, however, then a second boiling or other long cooking are unsuitable. Keep in mind that, while all of these storage and cooking considerations are important, what's most important is to choose a variety of whole fresh plant foods as the main focus of your menu!

## Add less fat, sugar, and salt

Besides choosing methods that maintain the nutrient content of food, we also suggest that you minimize the addition of extra fat, salt, and sugar. Both oils and sugar are partitioned foods and thus are generally low in vitamins, minerals, and fiber.

To illustrate the effect of cooking methods on nutritional content, let's compare homemade French fries to a baked potato. If you bring home a potato from a local farmers' market in September, keep it until December, then make it into French fries by peeling, slicing, washing, frying, and salting it, you will end up with a food that has a nutrient content more similar to potato chips than to a baked potato.

*Homemade French fries from one medium potato have twice as many calories, eighty times as much fat, and nineteen times as much salt as a medium baked potato.*

### Less fat

Keeping fat intake low is important, because fat adds to the caloric density of the diet (the amount of energy it contains), making maintenance of a healthy weight more difficult. More importantly, high fat intake, especially from animal-based foods, increases your risk of high blood cholesterol, heart disease, some types of cancer, and—when it contributes to excess weight—diabetes and hypertension. Considering the many benefits of a low-fat diet, we recommend that you experiment with cooking methods and try adapting recipes to reduce or remove the added fat to find new ways to make your food taste great!

### Less sugar

As most people know, minimizing the consumption of concentrated and refined sugar is now known to be important for many health reasons, besides sugar's long-known effects on dental caries. Adding sugar to the diet also reduces the amount of nutrient-rich food we eat. In other words, if we fill up on half a roll of Life Savers, we won't have room for a juicy orange. While the orange contains sugar, the sugar is in its native or whole food state. The orange is much preferable to the caloric equivalent of the Life Savers, because the orange also offers vitamins, fiber, and water. The Life Savers could be considered only sugar and some artificial flavors and colors.

And while it is true that sugar is a source of energy, whole foods, especially foods containing complex carbohydrates, are better sources of energy because they are packed with lots of other nutrients. High-sugar, empty-calorie foods are mostly a problem because of what they lack rather than what they contain.

*Less salt*

The amount of salt consumed is a concern for different reasons. It contains no calories and is in fact needed for proper functioning of the body. Why, then, is salt a problem? Problems occur when the intake of salt gets too high, which can happen all too easily, because the amount of salt needed by the body each day is less than half a teaspoon. For some people who are "salt-sensitive," meaning that their bodies are not very efficient at removing excess salt, too much salt can cause high blood pressure. For everyone, increased salt intake means an increased need for water to clean it out, an increased risk of bloating (water retention), and, more seriously, an increased risk of stomach and esophageal cancer.

You do have important control over the nutritional state of the food that you eat. Careful selection, storage, and preparation of your food can make a real difference in your nutritional health.

## Changing an animal-based recipe to a plant-based recipe

Occasionally you may want to change a favorite animal food–based recipe to a plant-based one. I have put together a list of possible food substitutions. You may know of other suggestions that work well. Use whatever makes the dish tasty for you and your companions. Be creative, and experiment with new spices and flavorings.

*Meat, poultry, or fish:*

Depending on the recipe and your food preferences, you can use favorite vegetables, beans, grains, or portabella mushrooms to replace these items. Other foods you can use as substititutions while transitioning to a whole foods, plant-based diet include tofu, which is available in varying consistencies, from very soft to extra firm (for slicing and crumbling). There is also seitan, a wheat product that comes in plain and spicy flavors, as well as soy hot dogs, veggie burgers, tempeh, and soy crumbles (similar to ground beef).

*Milk:*

When making a cream sauce or a pudding, I have found the best replacement to be soy milk. Otherwise, rice milk or any other type of milk substitute can be used in its place.

*Sugars, honey, or other sweeteners:*

When substituting for the sweetness of refined sugar, try concentrated pure fruit juice—specifically apple juice—maple syrup, or any of a wide variety of pureed fruits, including applesauce, bananas, preserves, and jams. Dried fruits, such as dates and raisins, work well for baking. Shredded coconut adds a sweet touch too.

*Fats and oils in main dishes or salads:*

Use vegetable stock, water, or wine for sautéing or frying. Bake instead of frying. Try oil-free salad dressings with a base of vegetable stock, water, or vinegar. When you eliminate added fat in cooking, you not only clean your arteries; you will find it easier to clean your dishes as well.

*Fats and oils used in baking cakes, cookies, and sweet breads:*

Prune paste is one of the best substitutes. It does not change the taste of the dish as much as other substitutions. Puree 1 cup of pitted prunes in a food processor with ½ cup of water. Substitute ⅓ the amount of prune paste for the amount of oil called for in the recipe (i.e., use ⅓ cup of prune paste to replace 1 cup of oil). Pureed bananas also work well in some recipes, but they do not hold moisture as successfully as the prune paste, and they distort the flavor.

*Salt:*

Depending on the recipe, seasonings such as onion, garlic, parsley, coriander, and celery seed can be used. Fresh onion, garlic, lemon juice, salsa, or any type of hot sauce can add zing without sodium. Low-sodium soy sauce is delicious in many recipes.

### TIPS AND SUGGESTIONS

Here are just a few of the tips and tricks I have learned over the years while making delicious, healthy, plant-based meals for my family and myself.

*Egg replacers:*

In this cookbook, when an egg substitute is called for in the ingredient list, I use the term "egg replacer." There are many different substitutes you may use for eggs. In most cases, you can use whatever is easiest or more convenient for you. Some examples of egg substitutes are (each measurement equals 1 egg): 1 tablespoon ground flaxseed mixed with 3 tablespoons water, ½ mashed banana, ¼ to ⅓ cup silken tofu, commercial egg replacer used according to the directions on the box, or ¼ cup applesauce.

*Sugar substitutes:*

For sweeteners, there are basically two categories: wet and dry. Here are a few examples of both:

*Wet*: agave nectar, maple syrup, brown rice syrup, molasses, evaporated cane juice.

*Dry*: brown sugar, date sugar, Sucanat, stevia.

The sweetness of each sweetener varies, so you may need to alter the amount according to taste. I recommend tasting your recipe along the way to determine if more or less is needed.

*Nondairy milks:*

As with many of the animal-product substitutes used in this cookbook, whatever kind you are most comfortable using is usually fine. Nondairy milks include soy, rice, almond, hemp, cashew, coconut, hazelnut, and many others. Experiment with a few different kinds to find one that works the best. Generally soy milk will produce a thicker product, and rice milk a thinner one.

## Brands we like

Here are some brands we like to use:

*Vegit*: An all-purpose seasoning, it can be used instead of bouillon to make broth, as a seasoning for soups, and anywhere you would add dried herbs or spices.

*Ener-G Egg Replacer*: A common commercial egg replacer that works really well.

*Mori-Nu*: This is a great brand of silken tofu. You can find it in most natural groceries or the health-food aisle of your grocery store. It is shelf-stable, so it won't be in the refrigerated section with the regular tofu.

## Chef's tools

Every cook has his or her own favorite kitchen tools. Here are some that I use on a regular basis:

*Sharp knife and cutting board*: This pair is a must-have in any plant-based kitchen. Everyone has their favorite knife and cutting board. The great thing about eating a plant-based diet is that you don't need to worry about which cutting board you are using because there is no fear of cross-contamination!

*Vegetable peeler*: In addition to its "regular job," the vegetable peeler also makes thin strips of vegetables for salads and other dishes. It's an easy way to "julienne" vegetables and also makes short work of peeling butternut squash.

*Crock-Pot*: Anyone familiar with this appliance will agree with me: it saves time! Many of the soups and stews in this cookbook can be made in the Crock-Pot. Prepare the ingredients and add them to the pot. You will have to adjust the cooking time, but it is a simple and easy way to make a hands-off meal.

*Griddle*: A pancake griddle isn't essential, but griddles are usually much larger than a regular frying pan, allowing you to make more pancakes at a time. Griddles are usually either electric, so you don't need the stove at all, or the kind that sits on top of more than one stove burner.

*Food processor*: This kitchen gadget has many uses. Depending on the different blades or attachments your processor has, you can use it to slice, dice, chop, grate, mix, and blend. It is really quite handy. A lot of the time, you can achieve the same results without one, but for some recipes, such as making hummus or pesto, it really is essential.

*Blender*: This kitchen staple comes in handy, especially when making smoothies or combining liquid ingredients.

### START YOUR OWN JOURNEY

The recipes in this cookbook are only a start. As you try them, make note of what works best for you. You may want to modify them, or you might keep them exactly as they are. Each person has his or her own preferences, but sometimes it's fun to experiment. Try new foods and spices you have never used before. When you find something that really works, use those same spices with other dishes. We have found it helpful to have fresh herbs, and each year we try to grow a different herb in our garden.

Don't forget to have fun. As I worked on this book with my sons, I found that we enjoyed our time together in the kitchen. Our lives can be so busy, especially for teenage boys who are active in sports and school events. Sometimes it's hard for all of us to be in the same place at the same time. But as we developed this cookbook, we found that we had quality time cooking together in the kitchen. Now when we are home together during the dinner hour, we all pitch in. It's fun. We pour our favorite beverages, a smoothie, or a juice, and then we cook. We turn on our music or NPR and find that we have some great discussions.

So as you begin this journey, invite your family to join you: your children, your parents, or both. To see pictures of recipes and get additional tips on how to prepare recipes in this cookbook, please visit our website at www.wholeplantscookbook.com.

Good luck and happy cooking!
LeAnne

SENSATIONAL HERB BREAD, p. 29

QUICK NO-FAT CRANBERRY BREAD, p. 27

PUMPKIN PANCAKES, p. 42

NATURE'S GRANOLA, p. 39

BLACKBERRY LEMON TEA CAKES, p. 23

ASPARAGUS CREPES, p. 94

CUCUMBER DILL DIP, p. 52

GARBANZO BEAN BURGER, p. 79

THAI WRAPS, p. 86

QUICK THREE-BEAN SOUP, p. 72

CILANTRO GREEN BEANS, p. 128

FRUIT SMOOTHIE, p. 36

# THE RECIPES

# BREADS AND MUFFINS

Banana Crumb Muffins
Blackberry Lemon Tea Cakes
Easy Pumpkin Muffins
Fiesta Corn Bread
Lemon Poppy Bread
Quick No-Fat Cranberry Bread
Raisin Walnut Bread
Sensational Herb Bread

# BANANA CRUMB MUFFINS

*Preparation time: 15–20 minutes*
*Baking time: 20 minutes*
*Makes 1 dozen muffins*

**1  cup whole wheat flour**
**¾  cup oat flour**
**1  teaspoon baking powder**
**1  teaspoon baking soda**
**1  teaspoon cinnamon**
**3  ripe bananas, mashed** (*TIP: you can mash the banana right in the mixing bowl*)
**⅔  cup vanilla soymilk (rice milk also works)**
**⅓  cup unsweetened applesauce**
**¼  cup dry sweetener**
**¼  cup chopped walnuts**

*For the topping:*
**6  tablespoons brown sugar**
**2  tablespoons cashew butter (optional)**
**½  teaspoon ground cinnamon**

1. Preheat oven to 375° F. Line a 12-cup muffin pan with paper liners.
2. Combine flours, baking powder, baking soda, and cinnamon in a medium-sized mixing bowl.
3. In a separate large bowl, mix together bananas, milk, applesauce, and dry sweetener.
4. Pour the dry ingredients into the wet mixture and stir until well mixed. Add the walnuts, and spoon the mixture into the muffin cups.
5. Mix together brown sugar, cashew butter, and cinnamon in a small bowl. Combine with a fork until crumbly. Press on top of muffins.
6. Bake in preheated oven for 18 to 20 minutes, or until a toothpick inserted into the center of a muffin comes out clean. Cool slightly before serving. ❋

*TIPS:*
- *If you want a crunchier streusel topping, add ¼ cup of raw oats.*
- *If you don't have oat flour on hand, you can make some by grinding raw oats in your food processor.*

# BLACKBERRY LEMON TEA CAKES

*Preparation time: 10 minutes*
*Baking time: 20 minutes*
*Makes 1 dozen cakes*

1   cup whole wheat flour
½   cup oat flour
⅓   cup dry sweetener
2   teaspoons baking powder
1   teaspoon grated lemon zest
½   cup plain soy yogurt
1   tablespoon lemon juice
2   egg replacers (4 teaspoons powdered Ener-G Egg Replacer
    and 6 tablespoons water)
1   cup blackberries
2   tablespoons white sugar for decoration (optional)

1. Preheat oven to 400° F. Line a 12-cup muffin pan with paper liners.
2. Combine flours, sweetener, baking powder, and zest in a medium bowl.
3. Mix together soy yogurt, lemon juice, and egg replacers in a separate bowl.
4. Pour the wet mixture into the dry mixture and stir until just moistened.
5. Gently fold in the blackberries.
6. Spoon mixture evenly into the prepared muffin cups.
7. Sprinkle sugar over the tops for decoration, if desired.
8. Bake in preheated oven for 18 to 20 minutes, or until a toothpick inserted into the center of a muffin comes out clean. Cool slightly before serving. ❋

*TIPS:*
- *Raspberries can be substituted for the blackberries in this recipe.*
- *These muffins are delicious served at breakfast.*

# EASY PUMPKIN MUFFINS

*Preparation time: 10 minutes*
*Baking time: 35–40 minutes*
*Makes 1 dozen muffins*

2  **cups whole wheat pastry flour**
½  **cup dry sweetener**
1  **tablespoon baking powder**
½  **teaspoon baking soda**
½  **teaspoon cinnamon**
¼  **teaspoon nutmeg**
1  **15-ounce can solid-pack pure pumpkin**
½  **cup water**
¼  **cup unsweetened applesauce**
½  **cup chopped walnuts**

1. Preheat the oven to 375° F. Line a 12-cup muffin pan with paper liners.
2. Mix together the flour, sweetener, baking powder, baking soda, cinnamon, and nutmeg in a large bowl. Add pumpkin, water, applesauce, and walnuts, and stir until just mixed.
3. Fill the prepared muffin cups to the top and bake 35 to 40 minutes, until the tops bounce back when lightly pressed. Remove from the oven and let stand 1 to 2 minutes; then remove the muffins from the pan. When cool, store in an airtight container. ❋

*TIPS:*
- *Store cooled muffins in an airtight container in the refrigerator. For longer-term storage, keep them in the freezer.*
- *Whole wheat pastry flour is ground from a softer variety of wheat than whole wheat all-purpose flour, so it makes lighter, finer-textured baked goods while retaining the bran, germ, and other nutrient-rich parts of the whole wheat berry. Look for whole wheat pastry flour in the baking section of natural food stores.*
- *You can substitute dried cranberries, currants, or other dried fruit for the raisins.*

# FIESTA CORN BREAD

*Preparation time: 1 hour*
*Baking Time: 45 minutes*
*Makes 9 servings*

| | |
|---|---|
| 1 | cup cornmeal |
| 1 | cup whole wheat flour |
| 1 | teaspoon baking powder |
| 1 | teaspoon baking soda |
| ½ | teaspoon sea salt |
| ½ | teaspoon tarragon |
| ¾ | cup corn, fresh off the cob or thawed |
| ⅓ | cup unsweetened applesauce |
| 2 | tablespoons maple syrup |
| 1 | egg replacer (2 teaspoons powdered Ener-G Egg Replacer and 3 tablespoons water) |
| 1⅓ cups soy milk | |

1. Preheat oven to 350° F.
2. Place the cornmeal, flour, baking powder, baking soda, salt, and tarragon in a large bowl and mix well.
3. Add the corn, applesauce, and maple syrup to the dry ingredients and mix. Add egg replacer and milk, and stir until everything is well mixed.
4. Pour into a 9 × 9 nonstick baking dish.
5. Bake for 45 minutes or until the top is firm and a knife inserted in the center comes out clean. Cool before serving. ❃

*TIPS:*
- *Serve with beans and cooked kale or other greens.*
- *If you want a more Italian herb flavor, add 1 teaspoon oregano and 1 teaspoon basil.*

# LEMON POPPY BREAD

*Preparation time: 10 minutes*
*Baking time: 55 minutes*
*Makes 2 loaves*

DIET
VARIETY

2 cups whole wheat pastry flour

¾ cup dry sweetener

¼ cup poppy seeds

1½ teaspoons baking soda

1½ teaspoons baking powder

1¼ cups soy milk

½ cup unsweetened applesauce

⅓ cup lemon juice

2 egg replacers (4 teaspoons powdered Ener-G Egg Replacer
 and 6 tablespoons water)

1½ teaspoons vanilla extract

1. Preheat oven to 350° F.
2. Stir together flour, sweetener, poppy seeds, baking soda, and baking powder in a large mixing bowl.
3. In a separate bowl, mix together soy milk, applesauce, lemon juice, egg replacers, and vanilla extract. Add the wet mixture to the flour mixture and stir until just combined.
4. Pour batter evenly into 9 × 5 nonstick loaf pans and bake for 45 to 50 minutes, or until a toothpick inserted into the center of the loaves comes out clean. Cool loaves in pans for 10 minutes before removing to a wire rack. ❋

*TIPS:*
- *For a stronger lemon flavor, add 1 teaspoon of lemon zest with the dry ingredients.*
- *If you prefer, chopped walnuts and dry, unsweetened coconut can also be added to this recipe.*

# QUICK NO-FAT CRANBERRY BREAD

*Preparation time: 15 minutes*
*Baking time: 1 hour*
*Makes 1 loaf*

2   cups whole wheat bread flour
¾   cup dry sweetener
1½ teaspoons baking powder
½   teaspoon baking soda
¾   cup orange juice
1   egg replacer (2 teaspoons powdered Ener-G Egg Replacer
     and 3 tablespoons water)
1½ cups fresh cranberries, coarsely chopped
½   cup chopped walnuts

1. Preheat oven to 350° F.
2. Mix together flour, dry sweetener, baking powder, and baking soda in a large bowl.
3. Stir in orange juice and egg replacer. Mix until well blended.
4. Fold in cranberries and nuts. Spread evenly in a nonstick bread pan.
5. Bake for approximately 1 hour or until toothpick inserted in the center comes out clean. Cool for 15 minutes before removing from the pan. ❋

*TIPS:*
- *If you do not have an egg replacer, you can substitute ¼ cup prune paste (to make a supply of prune paste, mix ½ cup prunes and 1 cup water).*
- *You can also use this recipe to make muffins and serve them for breakfast.*
- *This recipe is great for Thanksgiving and other holidays.*

# RAISIN WALNUT BREAD

*Preparation time: 5 minutes*
*Baking time: 1 hour*
*Makes 1 loaf*

1¾ cups soy or rice milk
2    tablespoons cider vinegar or distilled vinegar
2    cups whole wheat flour
1    cup unbleached flour
2    teaspoons baking soda
¼    cup brown sugar
1    small banana, mashed
1    cup raisins
½    cup walnuts

1. Preheat oven to 325° F. Mix the milk with the vinegar and set aside.
2. Combine the flours, baking soda, and brown sugar in a large mixing bowl. Add the milk mixture, banana, raisins, and walnuts. Stir just enough to mix. The batter will be fairly stiff and sticky.
3. Spoon into a 9 × 5 nonstick loaf pan and bake for 1 hour. Remove the pan from the oven and place on a rack to cool. ❋

*TIPS:*
• *Store flour, especially whole grain flour, in a cool, dark place.*

# SENSATIONAL HERB BREAD

*Preparation time: 1 hour and 15 minutes*
*Baking time: 35 minutes*
*Makes 1 loaf*

3  cups whole wheat flour
2  tablespoons mixed dried herbs (½ tablespoon each of
   sage, thyme, basil, and oregano)
1½ teaspoons dried packaged yeast
2  teaspoons molasses
1½ cups lukewarm water

1. Combine flour and herbs in a large mixing bowl. Stir in the yeast.
2. Make a well in the center of the flour and pour in the molasses and water. Mix by
   hand to make a soft, slightly wet dough. Knead until the dough leaves the sides of
   the bowl clean and feels elastic.
3. Place the dough in a nonstick bread pan, cover with oiled plastic wrap, and leave to
   double in a warm, draft-free place for about 1 hour.
4. Preheat oven to 400° F.
5. Bake for about 35 minutes. Test to see if bread is ready by tapping the top with your
   knuckles. Bread is done when it sounds hollow. ❋

*TIPS:*
- *Fresh herbs can also be used in this recipe. For a slightly different taste, rosemary and*
  *chives can be substituted for thyme and basil.*
- *This bread is great served with soup.*

# BREAKFAST DISHES

Blueberry Coffee Cake
Breakfast Home-Fry Hash
Favorite French Toast
Fruit Crepes
Fruit Smoothies
G-Mom's Oatmeal
Muesli
Nature's Granola
Our Favorite Breakfast Burrito
Panana Cakes
Pumpkin Pancakes
Scrambled Tofu
Scrumptious Apple-Filled Bagels

# BLUEBERRY COFFEE CAKE

*Preparation time: 10 minutes*
*Baking time: 25 minutes*
*Makes 9 servings*

DIET
VARIETY

1½ cups whole wheat flour
½   cup brown sugar
2    teaspoons baking powder
1½ teaspoons ground cinnamon
½   teaspoon baking soda
¼   teaspoon ground nutmeg
1    cup nondairy milk
4    tablespoons water
3    egg replacers (6 teaspoons powdered Ener-G Egg Replacer and 9 tablespoons water)
½   teaspoon vanilla extract
1    cup blueberries
¼   cup chopped walnuts

*For topping:*
3    tablespoons dry sweetener
2    tablespoons cashew butter
½   teaspoon ground cinnamon

1. Preheat oven to 350° F.
2. Combine flour, brown sugar, baking powder, cinnamon, baking soda, and nutmeg in a medium bowl.
3. Mix nondairy milk, water, egg replacers, and vanilla extract in a separate bowl.
4. Pour the wet mixture into the flour mixture and stir until smooth.
5. Spread batter into a 9 × 9 nonstick baking pan. Sprinkle blueberries and walnuts over the batter, and stir slightly so they stay on the top.
6. In a small bowl, combine the dry sweetener, cashew butter, and cinnamon. Mix with a fork, and sprinkle topping over batter.
7. Bake for 20 to 25 minutes, or until a toothpick inserted into the center of the cake comes out clean. Cool slightly before serving. ❉

# BREAKFAST HOME-FRY HASH

*Preparation time: 10 minutes*
*Cooking time: 30 minutes*
*Makes 4 servings*

DIET
VARIETY

4  large potatoes, scrubbed and sliced
½  cup water, maybe more
1  onion, thinly sliced
1  green pepper, diced
4  teaspoons light soy sauce or tamari
¼  teaspoon black pepper
6  cherry tomatoes, cut into quarters
2  green onions, thinly sliced

1. Cut the unpeeled potatoes into ½-inch cubes and steam them until just tender when pierced with a sharp knife, about 10 minutes. Remove from heat and set aside.
2. Heat ¼ cup of water in a large nonstick skillet over medium-high heat, and add the onions and green peppers. Cook, stirring frequently, until the water has evaporated and the onions begin to stick to the pan. Scrape the pan as you add another ¼ cup of water; then cook until the onions once again begin to stick. This will take about 12 minutes.
3. Add the diced potatoes and sprinkle with the soy sauce or tamari and black pepper. Cook, turning gently with a spatula, until the potatoes are golden brown.
4. Garnish with cherry tomatoes and green onions. ❋

*TIP:*
- *If you don't have time to go through this process, dice several large potatoes, sprinkle with your favorite seasoning (salt and garlic powder or onion powder), and bake in the oven for 20 minutes at 375° F.*

# FAVORITE FRENCH TOAST

*Preparation time: 20 minutes*
*Cooking time: 20 minutes*
*Makes 16 slices*

2 cups vanilla soy milk
5 tablespoons whole wheat flour
3 teaspoons dry sweetener
1½ teaspoons pumpkin pie spice
1 teaspoon vanilla extract
1 loaf sliced bread
Fresh fruit, fruit preserves, or syrup, for topping

1. Mix milk, flour, sweetener, pumpkin pie spice, and vanilla extract in a large mixing bowl to form batter.
2. Dip bread into batter and fry on both sides in lightly greased pan until golden brown.
3. Serve with fresh fruit, fruit preserves, or syrup. ❈

*TIPS:*
- *We like to use different types of breads for this recipe (raisin bread is good here).*
- *Instead of fresh fruit, you can use 2 cups of frozen fruit, heated over the stove with 1 cup water and thickened with corn starch and sugar, as a topping for this recipe.*

# FRUIT CREPES

*Preparation time: 10 minutes*
*Cooking time: 20 minutes*
*Makes 12 large crepes*

*For the crepes:*

| | |
|---|---|
| 1 | **cup whole wheat flour** |
| 1 | **teaspoon cinnamon** |
| 2 | **egg replacers (4 teaspoons powdered Ener-G Egg Replacer and 6 tablespoons water)** |
| 1¼ | **cups nondairy milk** |
| 1 | **teaspoon vanilla extract** |

1. Mix the flour and cinnamon in a medium bowl. Add egg replacers and stir gently. Slowly stir in milk and vanilla extract, beating with a wire whisk until batter is smooth. Batter should be very thin. Add more milk if needed.
2. Heat a nonstick skillet or crepe pan over medium heat until hot. Using a ¼ cup measure, distribute batter evenly over bottom of pan. Tilt and rotate the skillet until the thin layer is spread evenly. Cook the crepe until it is done on the bottom. Flip the crepe and cook briefly on the other side. Remove to a flat plate. Repeat this process with the remaining batter.
3. If the batter thickens while making the crepes, thin it with a little extra milk. ❈

*For the fruit filling (use any, all, or a combination thereof):*

**Strawberries, sliced**
**Blueberries**
**Peaches, sliced**
**Walnuts, finely chopped**
**Cinnamon**
**Maple syrup**

1. Mix together 2–3 cups of fresh fruit. Add ½ cup walnuts. Drizzle 2–3 tablespoons maple syrup on fruit, and mix.
2. Taking 1 crepe at a time, place 1–2 tablespoons fruit mixture on one side of the crepe. Fold the other side of the crepe over the fruit mixture. Drizzle with maple syrup and sprinkle with cinnamon. ❈

*TIPS:*
- *Although crepes are notorious for being hard to make, this is an easy and delicious recipe. The crepes come out perfect every time!*
- *My sons often add applesauce on top of these crepes.*

# FRUIT SMOOTHIES

*Preparation time: 5 minutes*
*Makes 3 cups*

DIET
VARIETY

*Banana blueberry:*

1  cup frozen banana chunks
1  cup frozen blueberries
¾  cup soy milk
2  tablespoons apple juice concentrate

1. Place all ingredients into a blender.
2. Blend on high speed, stopping the blender occasionally to move any unblended fruit toward the blades. For a thinner smoothie, add more milk. Serve immediately. ❋

*Mixed berry peach:*

1  10-ounce package frozen mixed berries
1  15-ounce can sliced peaches, drained
¾  cup soy milk
2  tablespoons apple juice concentrate

*Tropical strawberry:*

1  quart frozen strawberries
1  banana
2  peaches
1  cup orange-peach-mango juice
2  cups ice

*TIPS:*
- *Fruit smoothies have a nutritional advantage over fruit juices because they retain all the fiber that is left out when making juice.*
- *The secret to making a thick, rich-tasting smoothie is to use frozen fruit.*
- *Look for frozen berries in your supermarket, or freeze your own when they're in season.*

# G-MOM'S OATMEAL

*Preparation time: 8 minutes*
*Makes 3 servings*

DIET
VARIETY

**2  cups water**
**1  cup "old fashioned" oats**
**½ cup raisins**

1. Boil water, add oats and raisins, and stir until thick (2–3 minutes).

**½  cup blueberries**
**½  cup sliced strawberries**
**1–2 kiwis, peeled and diced**
    **Maple syrup**
    **Flaxseed**
    **Cinnamon, to taste**
    **Walnuts, chopped (optional)**

1. Place blueberries in the bottom of a serving bowl. Drizzle with maple syrup.
2. Pour cooked oatmeal mixture over the blueberries. Lay strawberries and kiwi on top of the oatmeal. Sprinkle generously with cinnamon and flaxseed, drizzle with maple syrup, and sprinkle with chopped walnuts. ❈

*TIPS:*
- *You can substitute any fresh fruit for the strawberries, blueberries, and kiwi. Bananas and peaches make good substitutes.*
- *My sister-in-law likes to pour rice milk over this oatmeal dish.*

# MUESLI

*Preparation time: 10 minutes*
*Makes 8 cups*

DIET
VARIETY

4½ cups rolled oats
1    cup raisins
½    cup toasted wheat germ
½    cup dried fruit, chopped
½    cup chopped walnuts
½    cup chopped almonds
½    cup unsweetened coconut (optional)
¼    cup raw sunflower seeds

1. Combine all ingredients in a large bowl. Mix well. Store in an airtight container. Muesli keeps for 2 months at room temperature. ❋

*TIPS:*
- *If you have never tried this granola-type breakfast, then you are in for a real treat.*
- *You can serve this with cold soy milk, or you can add soy milk and heat in the microwave to eat it warm.*
- *As with any cereal, adding fresh fruit (peaches, strawberries, or blueberries) makes it even more delicious.*
- *Feel free to add other flavors you like, such as cinnamon, nutmeg, vanilla, or honey.*

# NATURE'S GRANOLA

*Preparation time: 10 minutes*
*Baking time: 1½ hours*
*Makes 12 cups*

DIET
VARIETY

1    cup water
½    cup packed brown sugar
⅓    cup maple syrup
2    teaspoons vanilla extract
½    teaspoon ground cinnamon
¼    teaspoon ground nutmeg
4½   cups rolled oats
¾    cup wheat germ
1    cup slivered almonds
1    cup chopped cashews
1    cup shredded coconut
1    cup raisins
½    cup dried fruit, chopped

1. Preheat oven to 250° F. Line two baking sheets with parchment paper.
2. Add water, sugar, maple syrup, vanilla extract, cinnamon, and nutmeg to a large saucepan over medium heat. Cook 2–3 minutes, until sugar is dissolved.
3. Mix oats, wheat germ, almonds, cashews, and coconut in a separate bowl. Add wet mixture to dry, and mix until coated.
4. Thinly spread mixture on baking sheets.
5. Bake and stir every 15 minutes until golden brown, dry, and crunchy, about 1½–2 hours.
6. Let cool, and then place in a bowl. Add raisins and dried fruit. Keep in an airtight container. ✳

*TIPS:*
- *This is a delicious recipe that makes the perfect ready-to-eat snack! Store the granola in an airtight container for up to 3 weeks.*
- *You can also serve this granola with fresh seasonal fruit, soy milk, or soy yogurt. We love topping it with blackberries.*

# OUR FAVORITE BREAKFAST BURRITO

*Preparation time: 40 minutes*
*Makes 4 servings*

4   large potatoes, diced
    Onion powder and sea salt to taste
1   Scrambled Tofu recipe (p. 43)
1   15-ounce can black beans
1   package Daiya (nondairy) cheddar cheese (optional)
4   large flour tortillas
1   jar of your favorite salsa

1. Dice potatoes and bake on nonstick baking sheet for 25–30 minutes at 375° F. Season with onion powder and salt.
2. While potatoes are cooking, prepare the Scrambled Tofu recipe on p. 43.
3. Once potatoes and scrambled tofu are cooked, assemble burrito. In the center of the tortilla, place 4 heaping tablespoons of potatoes, top with 4 heaping tablespoons of tofu mixture, and then add 4 tablespoons of black beans. Sprinkle a handful of Daiya cheese on top of beans. Fold the bottom of burrito over, and then fold over both sides. Once burritos are assembled, place face down on nonstick baking tray.
4. Bake for 5 minutes at 375° F. Before serving, spoon 4 tablespoons of your favorite salsa on top. Serve immediately. ❀

*TIPS:*
- *Daiya nondairy cheddar cheese can be found in most health food stores.*
- *My sons love these burritos. We prepare them on the weekend and have them with a small fruit salad.*

# PANANA CAKES

*Preparation time: 25 minutes*
*Makes 4 servings*

1   cup whole wheat flour
1   cup oat flour
1   teaspoon baking soda
1   teaspoon baking powder
1   teaspoon cinnamon
½   banana, mashed
1   cup water
1   cup nondairy milk
2   egg replacers (4 teaspoons powdered Ener-G Egg Replacer
     and 6 tablespoons water)
2   tablespoons maple syrup

1. Combine flours, baking soda, baking powder, and cinnamon in a medium-sized
   mixing bowl.
2. In a separate bowl, mix mashed banana, water, milk, egg replacers, and maple syrup.
3. Combine the wet and dry ingredients, and stir just enough to remove any lumps.
   The batter should be pourable; if it seems too thick, add more milk.
4. Preheat a nonstick skillet or griddle. Using a ¼ cup measure, pour small amounts of
   batter onto the heated surface, and cook until the top bubbles. Turn with a spatula
   and cook the second side until golden brown. Serve immediately. ❋

*TIPS:*
- *Keep the cakes small. They are easier to turn.*
- *This is a delicious way to use up any bananas that are too ripe to eat on their own.*
- *Preheat the pan so that sprinkles of water dance on it, but not so hot that it smokes.*
- *Pancakes are best when served fresh and hot. Serve with fresh fruit, fruit preserves,
  applesauce, or syrup.*

# PUMPKIN PANCAKES

*Preparation time: 20 minutes*
*Makes 14 pancakes*

DIET
VARIETY

1 **cup whole wheat flour**
1 **cup oat flour**
1 **teaspoon baking soda**
1 **teaspoon baking powder**
½ **teaspoon ground cinnamon**
½ **teaspoon ground nutmeg**
½ **teaspoon ground ginger**
2 **egg replacers (4 teaspoons powdered Ener-G Egg Replacer**
  **and 6 tablespoons water)**
2 **cups nondairy milk**
1 **cup pumpkin (canned or pureed)**
5 **tablespoons maple syrup**
½ **teaspoon vanilla extract**

1. Preheat a nonstick skillet or griddle over medium-high heat.
2. Combine flours, baking soda, baking powder, cinnamon, nutmeg, and ginger in a large mixing bowl. Set aside.
3. In separate medium bowl, mix egg replacers, soy milk, pumpkin, maple syrup, and vanilla extract.
4. Combine the wet and dry ingredients and stir just enough to remove any lumps. The batter should be pourable; if it seems too thick, add more milk.
5. Use a ¼ cup or ⅓ cup measuring cup to measure and pour small amounts of batter onto the heated surface. Cook until top bubbles, about 2–3 minutes. Turn with a spatula and cook the second side until golden brown. Serve immediately. ❋

*TIPS:*
- *Use a good-quality nonstick skillet or griddle. Some pancakes may be cooked without any fat or oil; others may require a light misting of vegetable oil spray to prevent them from sticking.*
- *Pancakes are best when served fresh and hot. If you want to serve a whole batch at once, keep them warm by stacking them on an oven-proof plate in an oven on low heat while you finish the batter.*
- *Serve with fresh fruit, fruit preserves, applesauce, or syrup.*

# SCRAMBLED TOFU

*Preparation time: 20 minutes*
*Makes 4 servings*

DIET
VARIETY

½  large onion, diced
½  large carrot, grated
2  cloves garlic, minced (about 1½ teaspoons)
1  teaspoon low-sodium all-purpose Vegit brand seasoning,
   or 1 vegetable bouillon cube
1  teaspoon curry powder
1½ teaspoons light miso
1  14-ounce package firm silken tofu, crumbled
   **Sea salt and black pepper to taste**

1. Gently sauté onions, carrot, garlic, and Vegit or bouillon cube in ¼–½ cup water in a nonstick pan over medium-high heat until onions are translucent, about 5–7 minutes.
2. Reduce heat to medium and add curry powder, miso, and tofu. Cook, stirring occasionally, for about 10 minutes.
3. Add salt and pepper to taste. Serve hot. ❀

*TIPS:*
- *Vegit is a powdered, low-sodium form of vegetable bouillon. It can be found in health food stores as well as the health food section of most grocery stores.*
- *This recipe is also good with ½ teaspoon dill.*

# SCRUMPTIOUS APPLE-FILLED BAGELS

*Preparation time: 1 hour*
*Makes 16 bagels*

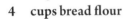

*For the bagels:*

| | |
|---|---|
| 4 | cups bread flour |
| 1 | tablespoon sugar |
| ½ | teaspoon sea salt |
| 2 | teaspoons instant yeast |
| 1½ | cups warm water |

*For the filling:*

| | |
|---|---|
| 3 | cups apples, diced finely (use a good cooking apple) |
| ½ | cup walnuts, chopped |
| ¾ | cup raisins |
| ⅓ | cup brown sugar |
| 1 | tablespoon cinnamon |

1. Mix all the bagel ingredients together in a bowl. Knead with your hands for 8–10 minutes, until smooth and elastic. Separate into 16 balls, cover them, and let them rise for 20 minutes.
2. While bagels are covered, prepare filling. Mix all ingredients in a medium-sized bowl and set aside.
3. After 20 minutes, roll out each ball to a diameter of about 3 inches. Place 1½ heaping tablespoons of filling into the center of each bagel. For each bagel, fold the edges together to form a half moon. Pinch the edges together with a fork. There should be no openings along the edge of the bagel.
4. Let your bagels rise on the counter for 15 minutes. Meanwhile, bring a gallon of water to a boil.
5. Add four bagels at a time to the boiling water. Flip bagels after 1½ minutes. Boil for a total of 3 minutes.
6. Place bagels on nonstick baking sheet.
7. Bake at 425° F for 20 minutes. ❈

*TIPS:*
- *This recipe is also great for plain bagels. Follow the bagel recipe, and after rolling into a ball, make a hole in the center and let it rise.*
- *These bagels are great prepared ahead of time and then served with a mug of hot cider.*

# APPETIZERS AND SALADS

Best Broccoli Salad

Black-Eyed Pea Salad

Ceviche Beans

Cole Slaw

Green Garden Mayonnaise

Couscous Salad

Cucumber Dill Dip

Crunchy Celery Salad with Olives

Ensalada Azteca

Fiesta Potato Salad

Fresh Tomato and Avocado Pasta Salad

Greek Salad with Nuts

Lemon Tahini Quinoa Salad

Lettuce Wraps

Mexican Jicama Salad

Samosas Baked to Perfection

Sesame Noodle Salad

Southwestern Salad

# BEST BROCCOLI SALAD

*Preparation time: 15 minutes*
*Chilling time: 2 hours*
*Makes 6 servings*

DIET
VARIETY

1   head fresh broccoli
½ cup craisins
¼ cup red onion, chopped
½ cup walnuts, chopped
2   tablespoons sugar
3   tablespoons rice vinegar
¾ cup Green Garden Mayonnaise (p. 50)
    Sea salt to taste
    Vegan bacon bits (optional)

1. Cut broccoli into bite-size pieces.
2. In salad bowl, add broccoli, craisins, red onion, and walnuts.
3. In separate bowl, mix sugar, rice vinegar, and mayonnaise.
4. Pour dressing mixture over broccoli mixture and toss to mix. Chill 2 hours, if time permits.
5. Before serving, add salt and vegan bacon bits (optional). ❋

*TIP:*
  • *Vegan bacon bits can be found in most health food stores.*

# BLACK-EYED PEA SALAD

*Preparation time: 10 minutes*
*Chilling time: 1–2 hours*
*Makes 8 servings*

DIET
VARIETY

1  **15-ounce can black-eyed peas, rinsed and drained**
2  **cups cooked brown rice**
2  **green onions, sliced**
1  **green pepper, diced**
1  **celery stalk, diced**
2  **small tomatoes, diced**
1  **tablespoon finely chopped fresh parsley**
6  **tablespoons lemon juice**
2  **tablespoons light soy sauce**
1  **teaspoon brown mustard**
¼  **teaspoon sea salt**
2  **cloves garlic, minced**

1. Combine the peas, rice, green onions, green pepper, celery, tomatoes, and parsley in a large bowl.
2. Mix lemon juice, soy sauce, mustard, salt, and garlic in a small bowl.
3. Pour dressing over the salad and toss to mix. Chill 1 to 2 hours if time permits. ❋

*TIPS:*
- *This salad will keep in the refrigerator for several days and is perfect when you need a quick snack or meal.*
- *For added color and variety, or to add interest to second-day leftovers, add 1 cup of fresh or frozen corn kernels and/or a sweet green or red pepper, chopped.*
- *You can also use fresh, frozen, or cooked, dried black-eyed peas in place of the canned peas (use 2 cups).*

# CEVICHE BEANS

*Preparation time: 25 minutes*
*Makes 3 cups*

DIET
VARIETY

1 medium red onion, diced
1 medium cucumber, diced
2 medium tomatoes, diced
¼ cup cilantro, chopped
2 limes, squeezed
1 can white beans, drained and rinsed
1 avocado, chopped
Pinch of sea salt
Baked tortilla chips

1. Combine onions, cucumbers, tomatoes, and cilantro in a medium-sized bowl.
2. Mix in beans, avocado, and lime juice.
3. Salt to taste.
4. Serve with baked tortilla chips crumbled on top. ❈

*TIP:*
- *Instead of crumbling the tortilla chips, you can keep the chips whole and serve this as a dip or salsa.*

# COLE SLAW

*Preparation time: 15 minutes*
*Makes 4 cups*

3  cups finely chopped cabbage
1  carrot, finely chopped
3  tablespoons vinegar
1  tablespoon sugar
2  tablespoons nondairy milk
1  tablespoon Green Garden Mayonnaise (see recipe on following page)
½  teaspoon dill
   Sea salt and black pepper to taste

DIET
VARIETY

1. Place cabbage and carrots in bowl.
2. Mix vinegar, sugar, milk, mayonnaise, and dill.
3. Add dressing to cabbage and carrots.
4. Add salt and black pepper. ❁

# GREEN GARDEN MAYONNAISE

*Preparation time: 10 minutes*
*Makes 1¼ cups*

8  ounces silken firm tofu
2  tablespoons lemon juice
1  teaspoon rice vinegar
½  teaspoon honey
¼  teaspoon sea salt
1  teaspoon nutritional yeast
½  teaspoon Dijon mustard

1. Blend all ingredients in a food processor until smooth. If you desire a thinner consistency, you may want to blend in a little water.
2. Refrigerate until ready to use. ❋

*TIPS:*
- *If you desire a garlic flavor or an onion flavor, you can add 1 teaspoon of minced garlic or 4 tablespoons of minced onion.*
- *Nutritional yeast, which can be purchased in health food stores, adds a slight nutty and cheesy flavor.*

# COUSCOUS SALAD

*Preparation time: 20 minutes*
*Makes 4 cups*

*For the salad:*

1¾   cup water
1     cup quick-cooking couscous
1     medium sweet red pepper, chopped
½    cup chopped cucumber
5     tablespoons minced green onion
¼    cup chopped black olives
1     large tomato, chopped
½    cup toasted pine nuts

*For the dressing:*

3     tablespoons fresh lemon juice
2     tablespoons water
¾    teaspoon dried oregano
¼    teaspoon dried mint
      Sea salt and black pepper to taste

1. In a small saucepan, bring the water to a boil. Remove from heat. Stir in the couscous. Let stand, covered, for 5 minutes. Fluff with a fork.
2. In a separate bowl, combine red pepper, cucumber, onion, olives, and tomato. Stir in couscous and toasted pine nuts.
3. In screw-top jar, combine lemon juice, water, oregano, mint, salt, and pepper. Screw top on and shake well. Drizzle on top of couscous. ❄

*TIP:*

• *This salad is delicious served over lettuce, with pita chips.*

# CUCUMBER DILL DIP

*Preparation time: 15 minutes*
*Chilling time: 2–3 hours*
*Makes 5 cups*

DIET
VARIETY

| | |
|---|---|
| 2 | small cucumbers |
| 1 | pound firm tofu |
| 3½ | tablespoons lemon juice |
| 2 | cloves garlic, peeled |
| ½ | teaspoon sea salt |
| 3 | tablespoons chopped parsley |
| 1 | teaspoon dill |
| ¼ | cup finely sliced red onion |

1. Peel and grate the cucumbers. Let stand 10 minutes.
2. In a blender or food processor, combine the tofu, lemon juice, garlic, salt, parsley, and dill. Blend until completely smooth.
3. Squeeze grated cucumber to remove excess moisture. Then place in a serving bowl with red onion. Add tofu mixture and stir to combine. Chill for 2 to 3 hours.
4. Serve with pita bread or your favorite baked cracker or chip. ❁

*TIPS:*
- *Reduced-fat tofu works well in most recipes and is available in most health food stores.*
- *Choose tofu that is fresh by checking the expiration date on the package.*

# CRUNCHY CELERY SALAD WITH OLIVES

*Preparation time: 15 minutes*
*Chilling time: 4 hours*
*Makes 6 cups*

DIET
VARIETY

6    stalks celery, diced
1    cucumber, seeded and diced
1    large carrot, shredded
3½ ounces chopped green olives
⅓    cup walnuts, chopped
5    tablespoons white wine vinegar
1    tablespoon oregano
1    teaspoon garlic powder
½    teaspoon dried rosemary
½    teaspoon dried thyme
4    cups macaroni, cooked
⅓    cup Green Garden Mayonnaise (p. 50)
     Sea salt and black pepper to taste

1. Combine celery, cucumber, carrot, olives, and walnuts in a medium salad bowl.
2. Mix vinegar, oregano, garlic powder, rosemary, and thyme. Pour over the vegetables and toss to coat.
3. Add cooked macaroni and mayonnaise.
4. Season with salt. If necessary, add more vinegar.
5. Cover and chill for at least 4 hours or overnight. ❈

*TIP:*
- *This salad is good served with Dante's Dominican Beans (p. 98).*

# ENSALADA AZTECA

*Preparation time: 15 minutes*
*Makes 10 generous cups*

2  15-ounce cans black beans, drained and rinsed
1  cup cooked brown rice
½  cup finely chopped red onion
1  green bell pepper, diced
1  red or yellow bell pepper, diced
2  tomatoes, diced
2  large avocados, diced
2  cups frozen corn, thawed
1  jalapeño, finely diced
¾  cup fresh cilantro, chopped
3  tablespoons seasoned rice vinegar
3  tablespoons apple cider vinegar or distilled vinegar
2  tablespoons lemon juice
2  cloves garlic, minced
2  teaspoons ground cumin
   Sea salt to taste

1. Combine beans, rice, onion, peppers, tomatoes, avocados, corn, jalapeño, and cilantro in a large salad bowl.
2. In a separate bowl, combine the vinegars, lemon juice, garlic, and cumin, and mix well.
3. Pour dressing over salad. Toss gently to mix. Add salt. ❁

*TIPS:*
- *Seasoned rice vinegar has a mild sweet-sour flavor that makes it a delicious salad dressing by itself or mixed with other ingredients.*
- *You may use lime juice instead of lemon juice. When given the option, I choose limes over lemons to juice because limes don't have seeds.*
- *Frozen corn can add great flavor, texture, and color to a variety of dishes. Use it straight from the bag; it's precooked and will thaw quickly.*

# FIESTA POTATO SALAD

*Preparation time: 40 minutes*
*Makes 6 cups*

DIET
VARIETY

1   **pound potatoes, peeled and diced**
1   **pound beets, diced**
1   **cup diced carrots**
7   **tablespoons Green Garden Mayonnaise (p. 50)**
1   **red onion, diced**
¼ **cup vinegar**
   **Sea salt to taste**

1. Boil potatoes, beets, and carrots in large saucepan. Drain vegetables and cool to room temperature. Place in a large bowl.
2. Add mayonnaise, onions, and vinegar to vegetables. Mix until vegetables are covered.
3. Season with salt. If necessary (depending on your preferences), add additional vinegar and/or mayonnaise. ✿

*TIP:*
- *This potato salad goes well with Dante's Dominican Beans (p. 98).*

# FRESH TOMATO AND AVOCADO PASTA SALAD

*Preparation time: 25 minutes*
*Makes 8 servings*

3  tablespoons Green Garden Mayonnaise (p. 50)
3  tablespoons diced red onions
1  teaspoon cumin
2½ cups diced tomatoes
1  15-ounce can chickpeas, drained and rinsed
½  cup torn basil leaves
2  avocados, diced
9  ounces whole wheat pasta shells
1½ cups cooked corn
   Sea salt to taste

1. Combine mayonnaise, red onions, and cumin in a large bowl. Add tomatoes, chickpeas, basil, and avocado, and toss to coat. Set aside.
2. Cook pasta according to package directions. Add corn 1 minute before end of cooking time. Drain and mix with mayonnaise-vegetable mixture. Serve immediately. ❋

*TIP:*
- *This pasta salad can also be prepared with cherry tomatoes and yellow peppers.*

# GREEK SALAD WITH NUTS

*Preparation time: 25 minutes*
*Makes 10 servings*

*For salad:*
- 8  cups salad greens
- 1  red onion, diced
- 1  red pepper, seeded and diced
- 1  yellow pepper, seeded and diced
- 3  medium tomatoes, diced
- 1  large cucumber, seeded and diced
- ¼  cup chopped black olives
- ¼  cup chopped pine nuts or walnuts
- Sea salt and black pepper to taste

1. Combine salad greens, onion, peppers, tomato, cucumber, olives, and nuts in a large salad bowl.

*For dressing:*
- ¼  cup diced green onions
- ¼  cup white wine vinegar
- 1  lemon, squeezed (about 3 tablespoons lemon juice)
- 2  tablespoons dried oregano
- 2  tablespoons Dijon mustard
- 2  tablespoons chopped capers
- 2  cloves garlic, minced
- 1  teaspoon dried basil

1. Mix all ingredients in a medium bowl.
2. Pour prepared dressing over salad and toss to coat. Season with salt and pepper to taste. ❋

*TIP:*
- *Capers are grown in the Mediterranean. They come from the caper shrub and are often consumed pickled and salted. They can be purchased in most grocery stores.*

# LEMON TAHINI QUINOA SALAD

*Preparation time: 20 minutes*
*Makes 10 cups*

1   cup quinoa, uncooked
2   cups water
½   red onion, finely diced
1   cup chopped broccoli
1   medium red pepper, seeded and diced
1   medium yellow pepper, seeded and diced
2   tomatoes, diced
1   15-ounce can garbanzo beans

1. Heat the water and quinoa until boiling in medium saucepan over high heat. Reduce heat to medium-low and simmer until water is absorbed and quinoa fluffs up, about 15 minutes. Quinoa is done when it is tender and there is a pop to each bite. Drain water and place quinoa in mixing bowl.
2. Add onion, broccoli, peppers, tomatoes, and garbanzo beans.

*For the sauce:*
¼   cup tahini
3   tablespoons fresh lemon juice
2   tablespoons hot water
2   tablespoons tamari
2   teaspoons sugar
½   teaspoon powdered garlic
    Sea salt to taste

1. While the quinoa is cooking, make the sauce. Whisk together all the ingredients.
2. Add the sauce to the cooked quinoa and vegetables.
3. Serve garnished with a bit of cilantro. ❁

*TIPS:*
• *For added color and variety, or to add interest to second-day leftovers, add 1 cup of fresh corn.*
• *This salad will keep in the refrigerator for several days and is perfect when you need a quick snack or meal.*

# LETTUCE WRAPS

*Preparation time: 15 minutes*
*Makes 6–10 wraps*

6–10 large Bibb lettuce leaves
3 cloves garlic, minced
1 tablespoon diced fresh ginger
½ medium onion, diced
2 large carrots, grated or thinly sliced
1 celery stalk, finely chopped
1 cup water chestnuts, diced
1 vegetable bouillon cube
2 tablespoons sesame seeds
8 ounces crumbled soy meat (or tofu)
2 tablespoons tamari or light soy sauce
½ cup dry-roasted peanuts
  Sea salt and black pepper to taste

1. Wash lettuce leaves, pat dry, and set aside.
2. In a medium skillet, add ½ cup water, garlic, ginger, onions, carrot, celery, water chestnuts, and bouillon cube. Cook over medium-high heat until onions are translucent.
3. Add sesame seeds, crumbled soy meat, and tamari. Stir fry for 1–2 minutes.
4. Remove from heat, stir in peanuts, and season with salt and pepper.
5. Take a whole lettuce leaf and place 2–3 tablespoons of filling in the center. Roll into a wrap and enjoy.

*TIPS:*
- *Any type of lettuce can be used in this recipe, as long as the lettuce leaves are big enough to be filled and rolled.*
- *These wraps are also delicious with a peanut dressing for dipping or drizzling:*

*Optional peanut dressing:*
  ¼ cup peanut butter
  ¼ to ½ cup water, as needed
  2 tablespoons soy sauce or tamari
  1 tablespoon brown rice vinegar
  1 teaspoon sesame seeds
  ½ teaspoon crushed garlic

1. Combine all ingredients in a blender or food processor, and pulse until creamy. ✻

# MEXICAN JICAMA SALAD

*Preparation time: 15 minutes*
*Makes 6 cups*

1 medium jicama root, diced (about 2 cups)
1 medium carrot, peeled and cut into 1-inch strips
1 large cucumber, thinly sliced
1 medium mango, diced
1 small sweet onion, thinly sliced (about ½ cup)
¼ cup cilantro, chopped
2 tablespoons seasoned rice vinegar
2 tablespoons lime juice
1 teaspoon stone-ground mustard
¼ teaspoon sea salt
  Pinch of cayenne pepper
  Pinch of paprika

1. Combine jicama, carrot, cucumber, mango, onion, and cilantro in a large salad bowl.
2. In a small bowl, mix the remaining ingredients. Pour over the vegetables and toss to mix. ❋

*TIPS:*
- *Add ½ cup of sliced radishes for added color and flavor.*
- *Seasoned rice vinegar makes a delicious salad dressing by itself, or use it as an addition to salad dressings in place of oil.*
- *Jicama is also known as the Mexican potato or the Mexican turnip. The root's exterior is yellow and papery, and the inside resembles a raw potato or pear. The flavor is sweet and starchy, and it is usually eaten raw.*

# SAMOSAS BAKED TO PERFECTION

*Preparation time: 20 minutes*
*Baking time: 12–15 minutes*
*Makes 6 samosas*

*Pastry:*

| | |
|---|---|
| 4 | cups bread flour |
| 1 | tablespoon sugar |
| ½ | teaspoon sea salt |
| 2 | teaspoons instant yeast |
| 1½ | cups warm water |

*Filling:*

| | |
|---|---|
| 1 | medium onion, chopped |
| 1 | jalapeño pepper, diced |
| 1 | tablespoon minced fresh ginger |
| 1 | teaspoon ground coriander |
| 1 | teaspoon ground cumin |
| ½ | teaspoon turmeric |
| 3 | medium potatoes, boiled, peeled, and diced |
| 1 | cup cooked peas |
| 1 | teaspoon sea salt |

1. To prepare pastry, mix all the pastry ingredients in a bowl. Knead with your hands for 8–10 minutes until smooth and elastic. Separate into 16 balls; cover and let rise for 20 minutes.
2. While pastry is covered, prepare filling by adding ½ cup water to a large skillet over medium-high heat. Add onion, pepper, and ginger, and sauté until onions are translucent.
3. Add coriander, cumin, and turmeric, and cook for 1 minute. Add potatoes, peas, and salt.
4. After 20 minutes, roll out each ball to a diameter of about 3 inches. Place 1½ heaping tablespoons of filling in the center. Fold pastry over and pinch edges together. There should be no openings along the edge.
5. Bake at 400° F for 15–20 minutes. ❁

*TIPS:*
- *Serve these with your favorite chutney or tomato sauce for topping or dipping.*
- *In place of peas, I often use shelled edamame.*

# SESAME NOODLE SALAD

*Preparation time: 35 minutes*
*Makes 6 servings*

DIET
VARIETY

| | |
|---|---|
| 8 | cups finely shredded green cabbage, about 1 medium-large head |
| 1½ | cups finely shredded red cabbage, about ½ small head |
| 2 | medium carrots, shredded |
| 1 | cup peanuts, crushed |
| ¼ | cup sesame seeds |
| ½ | medium onion, finely diced |
| 8 | ounces whole wheat linguini, cooked |
| 2 | tablespoons light soy sauce |
| 3 | tablespoons miso |
| 1 | tablespoon finely minced ginger |
| ⅔ | cup seasoned rice vinegar |
| 2 | tablespoons sugar or other dry sweetener |
| ½ | teaspoon black pepper |

1. Mix the cabbages and carrots together in a large salad bowl.
2. Add peanuts, sesame seeds, onions, and cooked linguini to cabbage.
3. Mix remaining ingredients. Pour over the salad. Toss to mix. ❋

# SOUTHWESTERN SALAD

*Preparation time: 15 minutes*
*Chilling time: 1 day*
*Makes 8 servings*

*Avocado dressing:*

2  **cloves garlic, minced**
¾  **cup soft avocado**
¼  **cup white wine**
2  **tablespoons lime juice**
1  **teaspoon Dijon mustard**
¼  **teaspoon sea salt**
¼  **teaspoon black pepper**

1. Combine all ingredients in a food processor. Pulse until well combined. Refrigerate overnight to blend flavors.

*Salad:*

8  **cups salad greens**
1  **small red onion, diced**
1  **green pepper, diced**
2  **tablespoons minced cilantro**
3  **medium tomatoes, diced**
1  **15-ounce can black beans, rinsed and drained**
1  **15-ounce can corn, drained**
1  **teaspoon oregano**
½  **teaspoon sea salt**
1  **cup baked tortilla chips, crushed**

1. Combine salad greens, onion, green pepper, cilantro, and tomatoes in a large salad bowl.
2. Heat beans and corn for 4 minutes over medium heat. Add oregano and salt. Add to salad right before serving, together with tortilla chips.
3. Add avocado dressing and toss to coat. ❋

# SOUPS

Aztec Soup
Coconut Corn Chowder
Dominican Chapea
German Sauerkraut Soup
Hearty Stew
Lentil Soup
Quick Three-Bean Soup
Seasoned Mushroom Soup
Spicy Pumpkin Soup
Thai Peanut Soup
Tomato Tortilla Soup

# AZTEC SOUP

*Preparation time: 30 minutes*
*Makes 4 quarts*

1   onion, chopped
4   cloves garlic, minced
¼   teaspoon cayenne pepper
1   tablespoon ground cumin
1   teaspoon ground coriander
1   teaspoon ground marjoram
½   cup diced celery
6   cups vegetable broth
4   cups diced white potatoes
4   cups frozen corn
4   tablespoons lime juice, separated
1   avocado, diced
1   large tomato, diced
¼   cup chopped fresh cilantro
    Sea salt and black pepper to taste

1. Sauté onion and garlic in ½ cup water in a soup pot over medium-high heat, until onions are soft. Add cayenne pepper, cumin, coriander, marjoram, and celery and cook for 1–2 minutes.

2. Add vegetable broth, potatoes, corn, and 3 tablespoons lime juice. Bring to a boil, then reduce heat and simmer for 15–20 minutes, until potatoes are cooked. Test for doneness by piercing with a fork. Season with salt and black pepper.

3. Meanwhile, in a separate bowl, combine avocado, tomato, cilantro, remaining 1 tablespoon lime juice, salt, and black pepper.

4. Pour hot soup into bowls and top with a rounded tablespoon of avocado salsa. ❈

*TIPS:*
- *Try using frozen white corn or hominy for extra sweetness and flavor.*
- *If you want a less spicy soup, only add a pinch of cayenne pepper.*
- *This soup is also good served with tortilla chips.*

# COCONUT CORN CHOWDER

*Preparation time: 20 minutes*
*Cooking time: 1 hour 20 minutes*
*Makes 6 quarts*

DIET
VARIETY

2　medium whole leeks, cleaned and chopped
4　medium carrots, chopped
4　cloves garlic, minced
1　jalapeño pepper, chopped
1　red pepper, chopped
1　yellow pepper, chopped
2　15-ounce cans garbanzo beans, rinsed and drained
3　cups frozen corn
2　14-ounce cans light coconut milk
2　cups water
　　Sea salt to taste

1. In a large soup pot or stock pot, sauté leeks, carrots, garlic, jalapeño, and peppers in
   ½ cup of water over medium-high heat until vegetables are tender.
2. Add the garbanzo beans, corn, coconut milk, and 2 cups water, and simmer for
   1 hour. Season with salt.
3. Serve hot. ❀

*TIPS:*
- *Slice and wash the leeks very carefully, as they have a tendency to be sandy.*
- *If you prefer a thicker soup, add more vegetables and reduce the water. For a thinner consistency, add more water or soy milk.*

# DOMINICAN CHAPEA

*Preparation time: 15 minutes*
*Cooking time: 1 hour*
*Makes 3 quarts*

6   cups water or vegetable stock, separated
1   medium onion, chopped
4   cloves garlic, minced
¼   cup fresh cilantro, chopped
2   large carrots, sliced
½   green pepper, diced
1½ cups rice, uncooked
1   cup chopped cabbage
1   can cooked pinto beans, rinsed and drained
1½ cups butternut squash, diced
4   tablespoons tomato paste
3   vegetable bouillon cubes
½   teaspoon sea salt

1. In large soup pot, add ½ cup water, onion, garlic, cilantro, carrots, and peppers. Cook over medium-high heat, stirring occasionally, until onions are translucent.
2. Add remaining water, rice, cabbage, pinto beans, squash, tomato paste, bouillon, and salt. Bring to a boil. Stir regularly to prevent sticking.
3. Once mixture comes to a boil, reduce temperature, cover, and cook for 20 minutes.
4. This soup is done when the rice is fully cooked. Add additional salt, if necessary. ❈

*TIPS:*
- *Serve topped with a few slices of avocados.*
- *If you prefer a thinner soup, add 1–2 additional cups of water.*

# GERMAN SAUERKRAUT SOUP

*Preparation time: 15 minutes*
*Cooking time: 30 minutes*
*Makes 4 quarts*

2  medium onions, diced

3  large carrots, chopped

3  celery ribs, chopped

4  cups vegetable broth

2  cups sliced fresh mushrooms

2  cups potatoes, peeled and cubed

1  can vegan cream of mushroom soup (Amy's brand makes a vegan version)

1  16-ounce can sauerkraut

2  tablespoons white vinegar

2  teaspoons dried dill weed

1  teaspoon sugar or other dry sweetener

¼  teaspoon black pepper

   Sea salt to taste

1. Place onions, carrots, and celery in a large pot. Add ½ cup vegetable broth and cook until onions are translucent.
2. Add remaining ingredients and simmer until potatoes are soft and tender. ✳

*TIPS:*
- *Add extra veggies if desired: red or green peppers, leeks, spinach, or corn.*
- *This recipe works well in a Crock-Pot.*

# HEARTY STEW

*Preparation time: 30 minutes*
*Cooking time: 20 minutes*
*Makes 3 quarts*

| | |
|---|---|
| 4 | cups vegetable stock |
| 1 | tablespoon soy sauce |
| 1 | onion, chopped |
| 1 | red bell pepper, diced |
| 4 | cloves garlic, minced |
| 4 | cups butternut or other winter squash (about 2 pounds), peeled, seeded, and cut into ½-inch cubes |
| 1 | medium potato, peeled and diced |
| 2 | 15-ounce jars of your favorite salsa, medium-hot |
| 1 | tablespoon dried oregano |
| 2 | zucchinis, chopped |
| 1 | 15-ounce can pinto beans |
| 1½ | cups corn |
| | Sea salt to taste |

1. Heat ½ cup vegetable stock and soy sauce in a large soup pot. Add onion, bell pepper, and garlic, and sauté over medium heat until the onion is soft and most of the water has evaporated.
2. Add the squash and potato to the pot, along with the salsa, remaining vegetable stock, and oregano. Cover and simmer until the squash is just tender when pierced with a fork, about 15 minutes.
3. Add the zucchini, pinto beans, and corn. Continue cooking another 10 minutes. Serve hot. ❀

*TIPS:*

- *Sautéing the onions in vegetable stock instead of oil reduces the fat in this dish, with no loss of flavor.*
- *You can substitute white corn or hominy for the regular corn, for extra sweetness and flavor.*
- *Canned beans can be replaced with dried beans that have been soaked and cooked.*
- *For a little heat, add ½ teaspoon crushed red pepper flakes.*
- *Use a vegetable peeler or potato peeler to peel the butternut squash. This will allow you to prepare the squash in half the time. Butternut squash is also available frozen.*

# LENTIL SOUP

*Preparation time: 10 minutes*
*Cooking time: 1 hour*
*Makes 3 quarts*

1  onion, chopped
2  cloves garlic, minced
6–8  cups water or vegetable stock
1  cup brown lentils, rinsed
1  large potato, peeled and diced
2  carrots, sliced
2  stalks celery, chopped
2  large tomatoes, diced
3  tablespoons dried oregano
1  teaspoon ground cumin
1  tablespoon curry powder
¼  teaspoon black pepper
¼  teaspoon red pepper flakes
   Sea salt to taste

1. In a large soup pot, sauté onions and garlic in ½ cup water over medium-high heat, until onions are translucent.
2. Add all remaining ingredients except salt and bring to a simmer. Cover and cook, stirring occasionally, until the lentils are tender, about 1 hour.
3. Add salt to taste. ✿

*TIPS:*
- *Adding salt at the end of a recipe allows you to use just the right amount.*
- *This soup can also be prepared in a Crock-Pot. If you start with boiling water, it will cook in 1–2 hours; with cold water, 5–6 hours.*
- *You can prepare a pot of this delicious soup and keep it on hand for quick meals. Reheat individual portions in the microwave and serve it with a salad of mixed greens and a slice of whole grain bread for a thoroughly nutritious and satisfying meal.*

# QUICK THREE-BEAN SOUP

*Preparation time: 10 minutes*
*Cooking time: 50 minutes*
*Makes 3 quarts*

1  medium onion, diced
4  cloves garlic, minced
1  15-ounce can black beans, rinsed and drained
1  15-ounce can red kidney beans, rinsed and drained
1  15-ounce can garbanzo beans, rinsed and drained
1  14-ounce can crushed tomatoes
1  16-ounce package frozen mixed vegetables
2  cups reduced-sodium vegetable broth
1  teaspoon chili powder
1  teaspoon black pepper
1  heaping tablespoon dried parsley

1. In a large soup pot, sauté onion and garlic in ¼ cup of water over medium-high heat until onions are slightly transparent.
2. Add remaining ingredients. Cover and cook on medium-low heat for 45 minutes. ❀

*TIPS:*
- *For variety, leafy greens like kale or chard and seasonal vegetables like zucchini, carrots, green beans, and corn are especially good in this recipe as a substitution for the frozen vegetables.*
- *This soup goes perfectly with Fiesta Cornbread (p. 25).*

# SEASONED MUSHROOM SOUP

*Preparation time: 30 minutes*
*Cooking time: 30 minutes*
*Makes 4 servings*

2   onions, chopped
1   pound mushrooms, cleaned and sliced
1   tablespoon paprika
1   teaspoon dried dill
1   teaspoon caraway seeds (optional)
    Black pepper to taste
3   tablespoons light soy sauce or tamari
1   cup water or vegetable stock
2   tablespoons unbleached flour
2   cups soy milk
1   tablespoon lemon juice
3   tablespoons red wine (optional)

1. Heat ½ cup of water in a large soup pot and add the onions. Cook over high heat, stirring often, until the onions are soft and all the water has evaporated, about 5 minutes. Add another ¼ cup of water, stir to loosen any bits of onion that have stuck to the pot, and continue cooking until most of the water has evaporated and onions begin to brown, about 3 minutes.
2. Add the sliced mushrooms, paprika, dill, and black pepper (and the caraway seeds, if using). Lower the heat slightly and cook 5 minutes more, stirring frequently.
3. Add the soy sauce or tamari and stock. Cover and simmer 10 minutes.
4. In a separate pan, mix 1 tablespoon water and flour to form a thick paste. Cook over medium heat, stirring constantly, for 1 minute. Then whisk in the soy milk and cook until steamy and slightly thickened.
5. Add the milk-flour mixture to the soup. Stir in the lemon juice (and wine, if using) just before serving. ❋

*TIPS:*
- *When choosing mushrooms, select those that are firm and unopened. Small mushrooms work best in this recipe.*
- *This soup is also delicious used as a sauce for pasta.*

# SPICY PUMPKIN SOUP

*Preparation time: 20 minutes*
*Cooking time: 20 minutes*
*Makes 2 quarts*

DIET
VARIETY

1 medium onion, chopped
2 medium carrots, chopped
1 stalk celery, chopped
½ teaspoon curry powder
½ teaspoon ground cumin
½ teaspoon ground coriander
½ teaspoon turmeric
1 cup water
2 teaspoons Vegit brand seasoning, or bouillon
1 cup soy milk
1 15-ounce can pumpkin puree
¼ teaspoon cayenne pepper
  Sea salt to taste

1. In a large soup pot, sauté onion, carrots, and celery in ½ cup water over medium-high heat, until vegetables are tender.
2. Stir in curry powder, cumin, coriander, and turmeric. Reduce heat to medium and cook for 1 additional minute.
3. Add water, Vegit or bouillon, milk, and pumpkin, and cook over medium heat for 15 minutes. Add cayenne; add salt to taste. Serve hot. ❁

*TIP:*
- *This is a fast, easy, delicious soup. If you prefer a smoother consistency, puree it with an immersion blender.*

# THAI PEANUT SOUP

*Preparation time: 15 minutes*
*Cooking time: 30 minutes*
*Makes 2 quarts*

½ medium onion, diced

1  stalk celery, diced

1  large carrot, diced

3–4  cloves garlic

½ sweet red pepper, seeded and chopped

1–2  jalapeño peppers, minced

2  tablespoons fresh ginger, diced

2  heads broccoli, chopped

2  cups chopped cabbage

1  tablespoon finely chopped lemongrass, white portion only

2  cups vegetable broth

1  15-ounce can unsweetened coconut milk

½ cup natural peanut butter

4  tablespoons tamari or light soy sauce

   Sea salt and black pepper to taste

1. In a large soup pot, sauté onion, celery, carrot, garlic, red pepper, ginger, broccoli, and cabbage over medium-high heat in 1 cup water until vegetables are soft, about 5 minutes. Add the lemongrass and cook for 1 minute.
2. Add vegetable broth, coconut milk, peanut butter, and tamari. Reduce heat to medium and stir until well combined. Cook about 5 minutes.
3. Season with salt and pepper. ✽

*TIPS:*
- *This is a fast and easy recipe. If you cannot find lemongrass, add a teaspoon of lemon juice.*
- *For a heartier soup, add 1 cup of diced sweet potatoes with the other vegetables.*

# TOMATO TORTILLA SOUP

*Preparation time: 15 minutes*
*Cooking time: 30 minutes*
*Makes 3 quarts*

| | |
|---|---|
| 1 | medium onion, diced |
| 3–4 | cloves garlic, minced |
| 1 | tablespoon minced jalapeño peppers |
| ⅓ | cup diced celery |
| 1¼ | cups corn |
| 1 | 28-ounce jar tomato sauce |
| 2 | cups vegetable broth |
| 1 | teaspoon ground cumin |
| 2 | tablespoons lime juice |
| 6 | small soft tortillas, cut into strips |
| | Sea salt to taste |
| 2 | tablespoons chopped cilantro |
| 1 | avocado, diced |

1. In a large soup pot, sauté onion, garlic, jalapeño, and celery in ¼ cup water over medium-high heat until onions are translucent, about 5 minutes.
2. Stir in corn, tomato sauce, and vegetable broth. Bring to a boil, then reduce heat and simmer for 10 minutes.
3. Add cumin, lime juice, and tortilla strips. Simmer for 2 minutes.
4. Season with salt. Serve garnished with cilantro and avocado. ❋

*TIPS:*
- *If you like a stronger cilantro taste, add ¼ cup of cilantro.*
- *If you want a heartier soup, add 1 cup diced sweet potatoes in step 1.*
- *This is a fast and easy recipe.*

# SANDWICHES

Delicious Eggless Sandwiches
Garbanzo Bean Burgers
Granola Fruit Wraps
Hummus Wraps
Ocean Chickpea Sandwiches
Pecan Ball Subs
Portabella Thyme Sandwiches
Tasty Tostados
Thai Wraps
Tomato Basil Pesto Sandwiches
Veggie Fajita Wraps
Veggie Subs

# DELICIOUS EGGLESS SANDWICHES

*Preparation time: 10 minutes*
*Makes 4 sandwiches*

12 ounces extra-firm tofu, drained and mashed
4  tablespoons green onions, finely diced
4  tablespoons Green Garden Mayonnaise (p. 50)
4  tablespoons dill pickle, diced
1  celery stalk, diced
1  medium carrot, finely grated in food processor
2  tablespoons rice vinegar
1  teaspoon ground mustard
1  teaspoon turmeric
½  teaspoon sea salt
8  slices whole wheat bread
4  leaves lettuce
4  slices tomato

1. Combine the tofu with the green onions, mayonnaise, pickles, celery, carrot, rice vinegar, mustard, turmeric, and salt in a large mixing bowl. Mix thoroughly.
2. Spread on whole wheat bread, and top with lettuce and tomato slices. ❋

*TIPS:*
- *Make sure you're actually getting whole wheat bread by reading the ingredient list: the first ingredient listed should be "whole wheat flour."*
- *Tofu varies greatly in flavor and texture, so sample several brands to find your favorite. Natural foods stores usually have a wider selection of tofu than supermarkets do. The freshest tofu has the best taste. Be sure to select fresh tofu by checking the expiration date on the package.*
- *Leaf lettuce is more flavorful and nutritious than iceberg lettuce.*
- *Mayonnaise is generally made with eggs and oil and is rich in fat, animal protein, and cholesterol. When purchasing premade mayonnaise, choose a soy mayonnaise that is not made with eggs, and read the labels to find one that is low in fat. Different brands vary widely in amount of fat per serving.*

# GARBANZO BEAN BURGERS

*Preparation time: 20 minutes*
*Chilling time: 1 hour 30 minutes*
*Cooking time: 12 minutes*
*Makes 6–8 burgers, depending on thickness*

| | |
|---|---|
| 1 | 15-ounce can chickpeas |
| 1 | small onion, peeled and quartered |
| 2 | large carrots |
| 2 | cups packed raw spinach |
| 1 | tablespoon soy milk |
| 2 | teaspoons tomato paste |
| 1 | tablespoon light soy sauce or tamari |
| ½ | teaspoon marjoram |
| 1 | teaspoon thyme |
| 1¼ | cups old-fashioned rolled oats (not quick-cooking) |
| | Sea salt and black pepper to taste |
| | Whole wheat flour, for coating |
| 6–8 | whole wheat burger buns |
| | Your favorite burger toppings |

1. Drain and rinse chickpeas. Place them in the bowl of a food processor with onion, carrots, and spinach. Blend until smooth. You may need to stop the processor periodically to scrape down the sides with a rubber spatula.

2. Put chickpea mixture in medium-sized bowl. Stir in milk, tomato paste, tamari or soy sauce, marjoram, and thyme.

3. Add oats to food processor, and pulse until smooth. Fold into chickpea mixture. Mixture should be thick and easily formed into 1-inch-thick patties. Form patties and chill for 30 minutes.

4. Spread a little whole wheat flour on a plate. Turn the chilled burgers in the flour so that they are coated on all sides. Refrigerate floured burgers at least 1 hour.

5. Fry burgers in a nonstick skillet over medium-high heat until browned on both sides, approximately 6 minutes per side. Burgers should firm up upon frying.

6. Serve on a bun with your favorite toppings. ❀

*TIPS:*
- *When making this recipe, I sometimes double it so I have extra for school lunches.*
- *I sometimes form the mixture into small balls, which I then stuff into pitas with shredded lettuce and diced tomatoes.*
- *These burgers are a festive green color and would be perfect for St. Patrick's Day!*

# GRANOLA FRUIT WRAPS

*Preparation time: 10 minutes*

**Large flour tortillas (or other sandwich wraps)**
**Low-fat peanut butter**
**Low-fat granola**
**Blueberries**
**Apples, peeled and diced**

1. Place tortilla in the microwave and heat for about 15 seconds.
2. Spread peanut butter down the middle of the tortilla in a 2-inch strip. Do not cover the entire tortilla.
3. Place two handfuls of granola on top of the peanut butter.
4. Place two medium handfuls of blueberries on top of the granola.
5. Placed the diced apples on top of the blueberries.
6. Fold the tortilla, first from the bottom and then from the sides, like a burrito. ❀

TIP:

- *This recipe makes the perfect almost-instant snack! My sons absolutely love this wrap. They eat it throughout the summer, especially when the local "u-pick" blueberry farm is open and we have an ample supply of blueberries. During the winter months, when the blueberries are more expensive and scarce, we use fresh red grapes and apples or frozen blueberries.*

# HUMMUS WRAPS

*Preparation time: 10 minutes*
*Makes 6–10 wraps*

1   **15-ounce can chickpeas, rinsed and drained**
2   **cloves garlic, minced**
¼   **cup tahini**
2   **tablespoons freshly squeezed lemon juice**
    **Sea salt, paprika, and cumin to taste**
6–10 **large tortillas**
    **Lettuce and tomato**

1.  Combine chickpeas, garlic, tahini, freshly squeezed lemon juice, sea salt, paprika, and cumin in the bowl of a food processor. Blend thoroughly.
2.  Spread on tortillas and top with lettuce and tomato slices. ❈

*TIP:*
- *You can flavor any hummus by adding your favorite vegetable or spice, such as roasted red peppers, horseradish, extra garlic, cayenne pepper, or sun-dried tomatoes.*

# OCEAN CHICKPEA SANDWICHES

*Preparation time: 10 minutes*
*Makes 4 sandwiches*

1 can chickpeas, drained and rinsed
5 tablespoons Green Garden Mayonnaise (p. 50)
1 tablespoon mustard
4 tablespoons diced dill pickle
4 tablespoons finely diced onion
1 celery stalk, diced
2 tablespoons rice vinegar
½ teaspoon kelp powder
8 slices whole wheat bread
4 leaves lettuce
4 slices tomato
Sea salt and black pepper to taste

1. Place chickpeas in food processor and pulse two times to roughly chop. Add mayonnaise, mustard, pickle, onion, celery, rice vinegar, kelp powder, salt, and pepper. Mix thoroughly.
2. Spread on whole wheat bread and top with lettuce and tomato slices. ❋

*TIPS:*
- *Kelp powder is found in health food stores and adds a great taste to this dish.*
- *If you like a stronger "seafood" flavor, add 2 tablespoons capers.*

SOUTHWESTERN SALAD, p. 63

BASIL PEPPER CORN, p. 124

TASTY TOSTADAS, p. 85

DANTE'S DOMINICAN BEANS, p. 98

LETTUCE WRAPS, p. 59

FRESH STRAWBERRY PIE, p. 148

TASTY POTATOES AND KALE, p. 137

PUMPKIN GNOCCHI WITH ITALIAN VEGETABLE SAUCE, p. 113

FRESH TOMATO AND AVOCADO PASTA SALAD, p. 56

NUTTY NOODLES WITH VEGETABLES, p. 111

CHEESE(LESS) CAKE WITH G-MOM'S NUTTY PIE CRUST, p. 144

NO-BAKE PEANUT BUTTER BARS, p. 153

# PECAN BALL SUBS

*Preparation time: 15 minutes*
*Baking time: 30 minutes*
*Makes 6 sandwiches*

1   **package extra-firm tofu**
½   **cup pecans**
½   **cup raw oats**
½   **cup coarsely chopped onion**
½   **cup finely shredded carrot**
2   **cloves garlic**
1   **teaspoon dried thyme**
1   **teaspoon dried tarragon**
2   **tablespoons light soy sauce or tamari**
½   **cup bulgur, cooked in 1 cup of water**
½   **cup tortilla crumbs or any nonfat bread crumb mixture**
1   **recipe Quick Marinara Sauce (p. 107) or your favorite spaghetti sauce**
6   **whole wheat submarine sandwich buns**

1. Preheat oven to 350° F.
2. In the bowl of a food processor, blend tofu, pecans, oats, onion, carrot, garlic, thyme, tarragon, and soy sauce. Place mixture in a large mixing bowl.
3. Mix in cooked bulgur and bread crumbs or tortilla crumbs.
4. Roll into balls about 2 inches in diameter and place on a baking sheet lined with parchment paper.
5. Bake for 40–45 minutes.
6. Place bulgur balls in sandwich buns and top with marinara sauce. ❈

*TIPS:*
- *This is a great recipe for a busy weekday, as almost all the ingredients go right in the food processor.*
- *Soy cheese is good on these sandwiches.*

# PORTABELLA THYME SANDWICHES

*Preparation time: 8 minutes*
*Cooking time: 10 minutes*
*Makes 4 sandwiches*

2 cloves garlic, minced or pressed
3 tablespoons balsamic vinegar
1 tablespoon water
½ teaspoon dried thyme
1 teaspoon Italian seasoning
  Sea salt and black pepper to taste
4 large portabella mushroom caps
4 whole wheat sandwich buns
1 tablespoon capers, drained
¼ cup Green Garden Mayonnaise (p. 50)
1 large tomato, sliced
4 leaves lettuce
1 medium red onion, thinly sliced

1. Turn on broiler and adjust rack so it is close to the heat source.
2. In a small mixing bowl, make the dressing by mixing garlic, vinegar, water, thyme, Italian seasoning, salt, and pepper.
3. Place the mushroom caps, bottom side up, in a shallow baking pan. Brush the caps with half of the dressing. Put the caps under the broiler and cook for 5 minutes.
4. Turn the caps over and broil for 4 more minutes. Toast the buns lightly.
5. Mix capers and mayonnaise. Spread mayonnaise mixture on the buns. Place mushroom caps on the buns and top with lettuce and tomato. ❈

*TIP:*
- *Portabella mushrooms have a unique flavor. Some people describe the mushroom as plain, but in this recipe the seasonings, together with the capers, make for a tasty sandwich.*

# TASTY TOSTADOS

*Preparation time: 15 minutes*
*Makes 4 servings*

1   15-ounce can pinto beans, rinsed and drained
4   thick gordita-style tortillas, heated
½ cup cabbage, finely grated
1   avocado, diced
½ cup salsa (you pick the heat)

1. Blend pinto beans in a food processor until smooth.
2. Heat beans in a skillet over medium heat for 5–6 minutes.
3. Heat a tortilla in an ungreased skillet until it is warm and soft. Spread bean mixture over the tortilla. Top with cabbage, avocado, and salsa. ❋

*TIPS:*
- *Be sure to select a tortilla made without lard.*
- *Nonfat refried beans can be used in place of pinto beans.*
- *Top with fresh cilantro, if desired.*
- *Additional toppings that go well on this dish are chopped onions, fresh tomatoes, and olives.*

# THAI WRAPS

*Preparation time: 20 minutes*
*Makes 4 wraps*

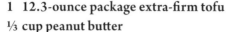

1   12.3-ounce package extra-firm tofu
⅓ cup peanut butter
4   tablespoons light soy sauce
1   tablespoon lime juice
⅛ teaspoon garlic powder
⅛ teaspoon cayenne pepper
¼ cup red bell pepper, chopped
¼ cup red onion, finely chopped
½ cup grated carrot
1   stalk celery, finely chopped
¼ cup chopped cilantro
¼ teaspoon powdered ginger
4   10-inch whole wheat tortillas, or 8 slices whole grain bread,
    or 4 pita pockets
4   leaves leaf lettuce

1. Drain tofu. Place in medium bowl and crumble with a fork.
2. Add peanut butter, soy sauce, lime juice, garlic powder, cayenne pepper, bell pepper, onion, carrot, celery, cilantro, and powdered ginger. Stir with a fork until well mixed.
3. Top tortillas with lettuce and then spread tofu mixture evenly over each lettuce leaf. Fold wrap like a burrito. ❄

*TIP:*
  • *This is a surprisingly tasty recipe. My sons and friends love these wraps.*

# TOMATO BASIL PESTO SANDWICHES

*Preparation time: 15 minutes*
*Makes 4 sandwiches*

2  cups fresh basil leaves, packed

⅓ cup water

½ cup pine nuts

3  medium-sized garlic cloves, minced
   Sea salt and black pepper to taste

8  slices of whole wheat bread

2  large tomatoes, sliced

1. Combine basil with pine nuts in a food processor. Pulse a few times. Add garlic, and pulse a few more times.
2. Slowly add water while the food processor is on. Add salt and pepper to taste.
3. Toast bread and spread with 2 tablespoons of pesto. Add sliced tomatoes and enjoy. ❀

# VEGGIE FAJITA WRAPS

*Preparation time: 25 minutes*
*Cooking time: 15 minutes*
*Makes 6 servings*

2  cloves garlic, minced
½ onion, sliced
2  green peppers, seeded and sliced
2  yellow peppers, seeded and sliced
2  large carrots, cut into thin strips
1  head broccoli, cut into florets
1  cup sliced mushrooms
3  green onions, chopped
1  tablespoon green chilies
   Lemon pepper and sea salt to taste
1  large tomato, diced
2  cups shredded lettuce (or raw spinach leaves)
1  large avocado, sliced
   Salsa, for topping
12  flour tortillas

1. In a large, lidded nonstick skillet over medium-high heat, sauté garlic and onion in ½ cup water. When onion turns translucent, add peppers, carrots, and broccoli. Cover and cook on medium heat for 2 minutes. Add mushrooms, green onions, and chilies. Re-cover and cook for 1 additional minute.
2. Season the vegetables with lemon pepper and salt. Stir well.
3. Cover and cook for 1–2 minutes until vegetables are tender.
4. Assemble your fajita: place a small amount of cooked vegetables in the center of your tortilla along with diced tomatoes, lettuce, avocado, and salsa. Roll and enjoy. ✻

*TIPS:*
- *Lemon pepper can be purchased with or without salt. Make sure you buy the variety without salt; then, if you desire, add the salt to your fajita separately.*
- *You can substitute or add additional vegetables to this recipe, depending on the season. Zucchini and yellow squash make good summertime additions.*
- *I often use romaine lettuce in place of iceberg lettuce.*

# VEGGIE SUBS

*Preparation time: 15 minutes*
*Makes 6 subs*

DIET
VARIETY

6  whole wheat submarine buns
1  large cucumber, sliced
1  large tomato, sliced
1  green bell pepper, seeded and sliced
1  red bell pepper, seeded and sliced
1  cup shredded carrot
2  cups leaf lettuce and/or raw spinach
1  large red onion, thinly sliced
1  large avocado, cut into slices or wedges
   Sliced pickles
1  cup sliced black olives (optional)
1  cup Green Garden Mayonnaise (p. 50)
⅓  cup red wine vinegar
   Oregano (optional)
   Sea salt and black pepper to taste

1. Slice the buns almost all the way through. Heat them briefly in a low-heat oven or toaster oven.
2. Spread mayonnaise on bun. Layer cucumber, tomato, peppers, carrot, lettuce, onion, avocado, pickles, and olives on top of mayonnaise. Drizzle with red wine vinegar. Add a bit of salt and pepper (and oregano, if using).
3. Close sandwich and serve immediately. ❀

*TIPS:*
- *You can also cut all the ingredients and place them on a plate. This allows each person to pick and choose his or her favorite combination.*
- *To add some heat, use diced jalapeños.*

# ENTRÉES

African Vegetables

Asparagus Crepes

Baked Stuffed Tomatoes with Couscous

Burger Salad

Coconut Curry Rice

Dante's Dominican Beans

Eggplant Parmesan

Fabulous Sweet Potato Enchiladas

Favorite Chili with Pasta

Fettuccine with Broccoli and Cashew Sauce

Green Corn Stew

Leafy Lentils

Leek Pie

Macaroni Squash

Mama's Kitchen Pasta with Quick Marinara Sauce

Masala's Chickpeas

Mom's Polenta with Rice and Beans

Moroccan Eggplant

Nutty Noodles with Vegetables

Portabellas with Spinach and Rice

Pumpkin Gnocchi with Italian Vegetable Sauce

Scrumptious Baked Vegetables with Fresh Spinach

Southwestern Calzones

## ENTREES *(continued)*

Spaghetti Squash with Savory Herbs
Tomatillo Tortilla Bake
Vegetable Lasagna
Vegetable Pot-Pie Stew
Zesty Bulgur Stew
Zucchini Crabless Cakes

# AFRICAN VEGETABLES

*Preparation time: 15 minutes*
*Cooking time: 25 minutes*
*Makes 10 servings*

1 medium onion, chopped
1 green pepper, chopped
4 cloves garlic, minced
1 tablespoon minced fresh ginger
¼ teaspoon cayenne pepper
1 tablespoon ground cumin
1 cup water plus ¼ cup, for sautéing
1 large sweet potato, peeled and cut into 1-inch cubes
1 package frozen chopped spinach (if using fresh, you may need to add more water)
8 ounces frozen corn
1 6-ounce can tomato paste
1 medium zucchini, peeled and sliced
¼ cup peanut butter
  Sea salt and black pepper to taste
4 cups hot cooked rice, for serving

1. In large soup pot, heat ¼ cup water. Add onion and peppers. Cook over high heat until onions and peppers are soft, about 5 minutes.
2. Reduce heat to medium. Add garlic, ginger, cayenne pepper, and cumin. Cook 1–2 minutes longer.
3. Add remaining 1 cup water, sweet potato, spinach, corn, tomato paste, and zucchini. Bring the mixture to a boil, reduce heat, cover, and simmer for 20 minutes or until potato is easily pricked with a fork. If necessary, add more water.
4. Add peanut butter, salt, and pepper. Cook over medium heat for 5–7 minutes.
5. Serve over cooked rice. ❋

*TIPS:*
- *This stew can also be served over millet.*
- *If desired, add chopped peanuts and chopped cilantro before serving.*

# ASPARAGUS CREPES

*Preparation time: 55 minutes*
*Cooking time: 20 minutes*
*Makes 6 crepes*

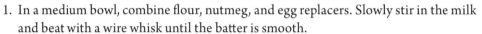

*For the crepes:*

1   cup whole wheat flour
1   teaspoon nutmeg
2   egg replacers (4 teaspoons powdered Ener-G Egg Replacer
    and 6 tablespoons water)
1½  cups plain nondairy milk

1. In a medium bowl, combine flour, nutmeg, and egg replacers. Slowly stir in the milk and beat with a wire whisk until the batter is smooth.
2. Drop a little less than ¼ cup batter onto a hot skillet or crepe pan. Tilt and rotate the skillet to distribute the batter evenly over the bottom of the pan. Cook the crepe until it is done on the bottom. Turn the crepe over and cook briefly on the other side. Repeat this process with the remaining batter.

*For the filling:*

3   cups chopped asparagus, cut into bite-sized pieces
3   cloves garlic, pressed
2   tablespoons lemon juice
¼   teaspoon dried tarragon
    Sea salt and black pepper to taste
½   cup raw cashews
1   teaspoon onion powder
½   teaspoon sea salt
1   can vegan cream of mushroom soup (Amy's brand makes a vegan version)

1. Preheat oven to 350° F. Sauté asparagus in ¼ cup water in a large skillet over medium-high heat until tender.
2. Add garlic, lemon juice, tarragon, and pepper. Sauté for 1 minute more. Set aside.
3. Place cashews, onion powder, and salt in the bowl of a food processor. Blend until smooth.
4. To assemble, place asparagus in center of crepe and add 2 tablespoons of cashew mixture. Roll up and place in a large baking dish. Top with mushroom soup.
5. Cover and bake for 15 minutes. Serve immediately. ❀

*TIP:*
• *You can also substitute green beans for the asparagus. Right before serving, top the crepes with sautéed mushrooms and garlic.*

# BAKED STUFFED TOMATOES WITH COUSCOUS

*Preparation time: 30 minutes*
*Cooking time: 20 minutes*
*Makes 4 servings*

4  large tomatoes
1  cup whole wheat couscous, cooked according to package directions
1  medium onion, diced
¼  cup water
2  cloves garlic, diced
2  teaspoons ground cumin
1  teaspoon paprika
½  teaspoon turmeric
1  vegetable bouillon cube
1  cup garbanzo beans
3  cups fresh spinach leaves, torn into small pieces
2  tablespoons raisins
2  tablespoons pine nuts
   Sea salt and black pepper to taste

1. Preheat oven to 350° F.
2. Cut the tomatoes in half and scoop out the insides. Turn the tomatoes upside down to drain while you prepare the stuffing.
3. Cook the couscous according to package directions. Set aside.
4. Place onion in a large skillet with water and cook over medium-high heat until onions are translucent.
5. Add garlic, cumin, paprika, turmeric, and bouillon. Cook for 1–2 minutes.
6. Add garbanzo beans, spinach, raisins, and pine nuts. Reduce heat to low and cook for 1–2 minutes.
7. Stir in couscous and season with salt and pepper.
8. Spoon the couscous mixture into the tomatoes and place in an 8 × 8 baking dish. If there is additional couscous, place in baking dish around the tomatoes.
9. Bake uncovered for 15–20 minutes. Serve hot. ❋

*TIP:*
- *It's best to use firm tomatoes, as they will hold up better after baking.*

# BURGER SALAD

*Preparation time: 25 minutes*
*Makes 4 servings*

*Dressing:*

1 cup water
1 cup tamari
¼ cup freshly grated ginger

*Salad:*

2 cups shredded lettuce
½ cup shredded purple cabbage
2 large carrots, cut in ½-inch chunks
1 large cucumber, diced
1 green pepper, seeded and cut in ½-inch chunks
½ red pepper, seeded and cut in ½-inch chunks
1 large tomato, cut in ½-inch chunks

*Other ingredients:*

2 cups cooked brown rice
4 Garbanzo Bean Burgers (p. 79) or your favorite vegan burgers

1. Mix water, tamari, and ginger. Store in refrigerator until ready to use.
2. Combine salad ingredients in a large mixing bowl. Toss to combine.
3. Heap each serving dish with salad. In the center, place 3 heaping tablespoons of rice and 1 burger. Sprinkle with ginger tamari dressing.
4. Serve immediately. ❀

*TIP:*

- *This recipe is adapted from a dish that we often ordered from one of my parents' favorite restaurants in Ithaca, New York, ABC Café, which is no longer in operation.*

# COCONUT CURRY RICE

*Preparation time: 15 minutes*
*Cooking time: 45 minutes*
*Makes 6 servings*

DIET
VARIETY

1   medium onion, diced
1   large green pepper, diced
2   tablespoons minced garlic
2   teaspoons ground cumin
2   teaspoons low-sodium Vegit brand seasoning or bouillon
1   15-ounce can pinto beans, drained and rinsed
1   13.5-ounce can unsweetened coconut milk
2½ cups water
6   ounces fresh spinach or 1 packet frozen spinach, thawed and drained
3   cups uncooked rice
    Sea salt to taste

1. Heat ¼ cup water in a large pot and cook the onion, pepper, and garlic over medium-high heat until vegetables are soft, about 5 minutes. Add cumin, Vegit or bouillon, and beans. Cook for 2 minutes, stirring occasionally.
2. Add coconut milk, water, spinach, and rice. Bring to a boil. Then reduce heat to low, cover, and cook for 30–35 minutes, stirring every 7–10 minutes until rice is cooked.
3. Season with salt. Serve hot. ❋

*TIPS:*
- *For this recipe, you can also use low-fat coconut milk. I have found that coconut milk can be purchased at specialty food stores, such as Asian or Latino markets, for a lower price than in traditional supermarkets.*
- *Black or red beans can be substituted for pinto beans.*

# DANTE'S DOMINICAN BEANS

*Preparation time: 25 minutes*
*Cooking time: 30 minutes*
*Makes 6 servings*

*For the beans:*

- 1 onion, diced
- 4 cloves garlic, minced or pressed
- 1 medium green pepper, diced
- ½ cup diced butternut squash
- ½ cup chopped cilantro
- ¼ cup chopped green olives (optional)
- 3 tablespoons tomato paste
- 2 vegetable bouillon cubes
- 2 cans pinto beans
  Sea salt to taste
- 4 cups cooked rice

*For the salad:*

- 6 cups sliced lettuce
- 2 cups cabbage, sliced into strips
- ¾ cup sliced cucumber
- ¾ cup sliced cooked beets
- 1 tomato, sliced
- 1 large avocado, sliced
  Balsamic rice vinegar and seasoned rice vinegar to taste

1. Heat ¼ cup water in a large stock pot and sauté the onion and garlic over medium-high heat until soft, about 5 minutes. Add the green pepper, squash, cilantro, olives, tomato paste, and bouillon. Cook for 2 minutes, stirring.
2. Add 1 cup water and the beans. Bring to a simmer and cook, uncovered, for 25 minutes. Season with salt.
3. While the beans are cooking, make the salad. In a large mixing bowl, combine all the vegetables. Toss with vinegars to coat.
4. Serve beans over rice and top with salad. ❀

*TIPS:*
- *Black or red beans can be substituted for the pinto beans.*
- *To save time, you can use frozen butternut squash.*
- *What really makes this dish is the salad served on top. The crunchy freshness of the vegetables and the tanginess of the dressing make for a perfect combination.*

# EGGPLANT PARMESAN

*Preparation time: 30 minutes*
*Cooking time: 1 hour 30 minutes*
*Makes 8–10 servings*

½ cup whole wheat pastry flour

½ cup soy milk

1 cup Italian bread crumbs

1 large eggplant, peeled, sliced ¼- to ½-inch thick, lengthwise

2 28-ounce jars of marinara sauce (or a double batch of Quick
   Marinara Sauce, p. 107)

1 10-ounce package whole wheat spaghetti or other long noodles, cooked

1. Preheat oven to 350° F.
2. Place pastry flour in a shallow bowl. Pour milk in a second shallow bowl. Place bread crumbs in a third shallow bowl. Bread eggplant slices by first dredging each slice in the flour, then covering with milk, and finally covering with bread crumbs. You may need to add more flour, milk, or bread crumbs depending on the number of slices your eggplant yields.
3. Place breaded slices on a parchment-lined baking sheet. Bake for 30 minutes, until brown, turning once halfway through. Remove from oven, but keep oven temperature at 350° F.
4. Spread five tablespoons marinara sauce over bottom of a 3-quart baking dish. Layer with ⅓ of the spaghetti or other noodles, followed by half of the eggplant slices and another layer of marinara. Top with another ⅓ of noodles, then add remaining eggplant slices, and cover with marinara sauce. Finish with remaining noodles and remaining sauce.
5. Cover with foil and bake for 1 hour. Wait for 10 minutes before serving. ❊

*TIPS:*
- *A low-fat, low-sodium bread crumb called Ian's Panko Bread Crumbs can be purchased in health food stores.*
- *You may want to serve this with additional marinara sauce.*

# FABULOUS SWEET POTATO ENCHILADAS

*Preparation time: 15 minutes*
*Cooking time: 40 minutes*
*Makes 8 servings*

| | |
|---|---|
| ½ | cup water |
| 1 | medium onion, diced |
| 5 | cloves garlic, minced |
| 1 | teaspoon coriander |
| 2 | teaspoons ground cumin |
| ¼ | teaspoon cayenne pepper |
| 2 | cups fresh spinach, chopped |
| 2 | cups black beans, chopped in a food processor |
| 4 | tablespoons soy sauce |
| 3 | cups cooked, mashed sweet potatoes |
| 1 | package vegan cheese (optional) |
| 12 | corn tortillas |
| 1 | jar of your favorite salsa |

1. Preheat oven to 350° F.
2. Heat water in a medium skillet over medium-high heat. Add onion and garlic. Sauté until onion is translucent. Add coriander, cumin, and pepper. Cook for 1 minute, stirring constantly.
3. Add spinach, black beans, soy sauce, and mashed sweet potatoes.
4. Add salt and additional cayenne pepper to taste. Continue cooking until mixture is heated through.
5. Place ¼ cup mixture in the center of each tortilla (and vegan cheese, if using). Roll into a burrito and place in a baking dish.
6. Once all the burritos are assembled, pour your favorite salsa on top and cover with aluminum foil.
7. Bake for 25 minutes. ❈

*TIP:*
- *You may want to serve this with additional salsa.*

# FAVORITE CHILI WITH PASTA

*Preparation time: 15 minutes*
*Cooking time: 20 minutes*
*Makes 8 servings*

8   ounces whole wheat pasta spirals
1   onion, chopped
3   cloves garlic, minced
1   vegetable bouillon cube
2   tablespoons oregano
1   tablespoon chili powder
¼   teaspoon cayenne pepper
1   small green pepper, diced
1   large carrot, grated
1   15-ounce can diced tomatoes
2   15-ounce cans kidney beans
1   15-ounce package frozen corn
    Sea salt to taste

1. Cook the pasta in boiling water until tender. Drain and rinse under hot water, then set aside.
2. Heat ½ cup water in a large pot. Add onion, garlic, bouillon, oregano, chili powder, and cayenne. Cook until the onion is soft, about 3 minutes.
3. Add green pepper, carrot, diced tomatoes, kidney beans, corn, and an additional ½ cup water. Stir to mix. Simmer over medium heat, stirring occasionally, for 20 minutes.
4. Add the cooked pasta and check the seasonings. Add more chili powder if a spicier dish is desired. ❀

*TIPS:*
* *Pinto beans or black beans may be substituted for the kidney beans.*
* *Substituting fresh sweet corn cut off the cob for frozen corn takes a bit more time but adds a deliciously sweet flavor to this meal.*

# FETTUCCINE WITH BROCCOLI AND CASHEW SAUCE

*Tom Frougee!*

*Preparation time: 25 minutes*
*Cooking time: 20 minutes*
*Makes 6 servings*

DIET
VARIETY

1  pound broccoli, cut into florets (and stems into rounds)
8  ounces whole wheat fettuccine
6  large cloves garlic, minced
½  cup raw cashews, processed until smooth in a food processor
½  cup soy milk
1  tablespoon miso
1  teaspoon ground mustard
¼  teaspoon red pepper flakes or pinch cayenne pepper
¼  teaspoon sea salt

1. Steam broccoli over boiling water until it is just tender, about 5 minutes. It should be bright green and still slightly crisp. Drain and set aside.
2. Cook fettuccine in boiling water until it is just tender. Drain and rinse quickly.
3. While the fettuccine is cooking, heat 4 tablespoons water in a large skillet over medium-high heat. Sauté the garlic about 3 minutes; add cashews, milk, miso, mustard, and red pepper flakes or cayenne. Cook over medium heat for 7 minutes.
4. Spread the fettuccine on a large platter, top with broccoli, and add sauce. Serve immediately. ❈

*TIPS:*
- *Be sure to use the broccoli stems. They are crunchy and delicious.*
- *For a cheesier flavor, add 2–4 tablespoons of nutritional yeast to cashew sauce.*
- *For extra flavor, use tomato basil fettuccine, or try a wheatless fettuccine such as artichoke or corn.*

# GREEN CORN STEW

*Preparation time: 20 minutes*
*Cooking time: 45 minutes*
*Makes 6–8 servings*

1    large onion, chopped
3    cloves garlic, minced
¼    teaspoon cayenne pepper
4    cups water
2    tablespoons Vegit brand seasoning or bouillon
6    ears of corn, shaved (about 6 cups kernels)
1    large potato, diced
2½ cups tomatillos, husked and chopped
3    jalapeño peppers, seeded and coarsely chopped
¼    cup chopped cilantro
     Sea salt to taste

1. In a soup pot, sauté onion in ¼ cup water over medium heat, stirring frequently. Stir in garlic and cayenne pepper. Cook for 1–3 minutes, until garlic is fragrant.
2. Add water and Vegit or bouillon. Bring to a boil and stir in corn and potato. Reduce heat and simmer for 20 to 25 minutes until potato and corn are cooked. Potatoes are done when they are easily pierced with a fork.
3. Add tomatillos and jalapeño peppers. Cook about 5 minutes, until tomatillos are tender.
4. Add cilantro and season with salt. Simmer for 5 more minutes.
5. Serve as is or on top of rice. ❋

*TIPS:*
- *Tomatillos can be bought in most grocery stores; they add a wonderful flavor.*
- *The final consistency of this recipe should be thicker than a soup, more like a stew.*

# LEAFY LENTILS

*Preparation time: 30 minutes*
*Cooking time: 55 minutes*
*Makes 4–6 servings*

1   cup uncooked lentils
2–3  cups vegetable stock
1   large onion, diced
1   tablespoon minced garlic
3   tablespoons dried oregano
2   cups diced tomatoes
4   tablespoons tomato paste
14 ounces chopped spinach, fresh or frozen
1   tablespoon balsamic vinegar
    Sea salt and black pepper to taste
4   cups cooked brown rice, for serving

1. Place lentils in a large saucepan with 2 cups vegetable stock. Bring to a boil over medium heat, then reduce heat and simmer for 20–30 minutes until lentils are tender. If needed, add additional vegetable stock. When lentils are cooked, drain and set aside.
2. In a large saucepan, sauté onion in 2 tablespoons of water over medium heat, until softened. Add garlic, oregano, tomatoes, tomato paste, and cooked lentils, and cook for 4–5 minutes. Add spinach. Cover and cook until spinach is wilted, 3–4 minutes.
3. Add vinegar and season with salt and pepper. Serve immediately over a bed of brown rice. ✽

# LEEK PIE

*Preparation time: 45 minutes*
*Cooking time: 45 minutes*
*Makes 4–6 servings*

*For the crust:*

3  medium potatoes, grated
¼  teaspoon sea salt
¼  teaspoon black pepper

*For the filling:*

3  medium leeks, chopped (about 4 cups)
3  cloves garlic, minced
1  pound extra-firm tofu, drained and crumbled
2  tablespoons lemon juice
1  teaspoon sea salt
1  cup whole wheat bread crumbs
¼  cup fresh basil
1  cup sliced mushrooms
½  cup chopped sun-dried tomatoes (avoid the kind packed in oil)
1  can of chopped black olives (optional)

*Crust:*

1. Preheat oven to 350° F. Wash and grate potatoes. Squeeze grated potatoes and drain moisture from them. Season with salt and pepper.
2. Spread and pat potatoes evenly onto a greased pie plate.
3. Bake the potato crust until golden brown. Remove from the oven.

*Filling:*

1. Sauté leeks and garlic in ¼ cup water over medium-high heat, until leeks are tender. Remove from heat and set aside.
2. In a large mixing bowl, combine crumbled tofu, lemon juice, salt, bread crumbs, basil, mushrooms, sun-dried tomatoes, and olives, if using. Gently fold in the leeks.
3. Spoon filling into crust and bake for 40 minutes. ❀

*TIPS:*

- *Wash leeks thoroughly, as leeks tend to be sandy inside.*
- *Be sure to use bread crumbs that are 100 percent whole wheat. Your bread crumbs are only as good as the bread you use.*

# MACARONI SQUASH

*Preparation time: 15 minutes*
*Cooking time: 15 minutes*
*Makes 4 servings*

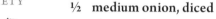

2½ cups cooked whole wheat macaroni
½   medium onion, diced
1    clove garlic, minced
1    cup cooked butternut squash, mashed
¾   cup raw cashews, pureed
½   cup soy milk
2    tablespoons Vegit brand seasoning or bouillon
    Sea salt to taste

1. Preheat oven to 350° F.
2. Place cooked macaroni in a large mixing bowl and set aside.
3. Sauté onion and garlic with a little water in a large skillet over medium-high heat. Cook until onions are translucent, about 5 minutes. Add squash, cashews, soy milk, Vegit or bouillon, and salt. Mix well and cook until just heated through.
4. Add to macaroni and mix well.
5. Pour macaroni mixture into a casserole dish, cover with foil, and bake for 15 minutes. ❋

*TIPS:*
- *Butternut squash can be purchased both in the frozen food section and in the produce section.*
- *Brown rice macaroni can be substituted for whole wheat macaroni.*

# MAMA'S KITCHEN PASTA WITH QUICK MARINARA SAUCE

*Preparation time: 25 minutes*
*Makes 4 servings*

DIET
VARIETY

⅓ **cup water**
5 **cloves garlic, minced**
1 **medium onion, diced**
4 **cups diced tomatoes**
2 **rounded tablespoons tomato paste**
6 **leaves fresh basil, chopped**
1 **tablespoon oregano**
  **Sea salt and black pepper to taste**
1 **cup vegan beef soy crumbles (optional)**
1 **pound of your favorite cooked pasta**

1. Place the water in a large skillet. Add garlic and onion. Sauté on high heat until onion is translucent.
2. Add tomatoes, tomato paste, basil, and oregano. Bring to a boil. Add salt and pepper. Then add soy crumbles, if desired.
3. Lower heat, cover, and simmer for 25 minutes.
4. Serve sauce over your favorite cooked pasta. ❋

# MASALA'S CHICKPEAS

*Preparation time: 15–20 minutes*
*Cooking time: 25 minutes*
*Makes 6–8 servings*

DIET
VARIETY

1½  cups chopped onion
2    tablespoons minced garlic
2    tablespoons minced fresh ginger
1    tablespoon turmeric
1    teaspoon coriander
1    teaspoon ground cumin
½    teaspoon garam masala
2    cups diced tomatoes
2    tablespoons tomato paste
     Sea salt to taste
1    teaspoon cayenne pepper (or less)
2    15-ounce cans chickpeas, drained and rinsed
¾    cup soy milk
½    teaspoon lemon juice
4    cups cooked rice, for serving

1. In a large skillet, sauté onion over medium heat with ½ cup water, stirring frequently, until onions become translucent. Stir in garlic, ginger, turmeric, coriander, cumin, and garam masala. Cook for 5 minutes.
2. Stir in diced tomatoes, tomato paste, salt, and cayenne pepper, and cook for 3–4 minutes. Stir in chickpeas, soy milk, and lemon juice. Cover and cook 8–10 minutes on low heat.
3. Serve on top of rice. ❋

*TIPS:*
- *Coconut milk adds a nice flavor to this dish, but you can eliminate this ingredient if you choose.*
- *The final consistency of this recipe should be thicker than a soup, more like a stew, and can be served with warmed pita bread.*

# MOM'S POLENTA WITH RICE AND BEANS

*Preparation time: 30 minutes*
*Cooking time: 1 hour*
*Makes 6 servings*

2   cups water
¾   cup polenta
¼   teaspoon sea salt

1. Place water, polenta, and salt in a medium saucepan. Bring to a boil and cook for 10–12 minutes, until polenta pulls away from the sides of the pan. Transfer to large pie dish and spread over bottom and sides of dish. Set aside.

1   small onion, diced
3   cloves garlic, minced or pressed
1   14.5-ounce can diced tomatoes
2   cups vegetable broth (I like Pacific brand—low sodium and no fat)
1   tablespoon chili powder
1   cup short-grain brown rice (sticks together better)
1   15.5-ounce can black beans, drained and rinsed
½   cup salsa
1   avocado

1. Place onion, garlic, tomatoes, broth, chili powder, and rice in rice cooker or pan. Cook rice until all liquid is gone and rice is tender (about 45 minutes).
2. Stir black beans into the rice. Spread rice-bean mixture on top of polenta.
3. Spread salsa on top of rice mixture.
4. Bake at 350° F for 30 minutes.
5. Remove from oven and set aside for 5–10 minutes.
6. Dice avocado and toss with lemon juice and garlic powder.
7. Arrange diced, seasoned avocado on top of dish. ❁

# MOROCCAN EGGPLANT

*Preparation time: 20 minutes*
*Cooking time: 30 minutes*
*Makes 6 servings*

1 medium onion, chopped

4 cloves garlic, pressed

1 teaspoon ground cumin

2 eggplants, diced (about 7 cups)

½ large green pepper, seeded and diced

½ large red pepper, seeded and diced

½ yellow pepper, seeded and diced

1 large carrot, grated

2 teaspoons turmeric

½ teaspoon curry powder

½ teaspoon garam masala

½ cup diced tomato

4 tablespoons tomato paste

2 cups vegetable broth

Pinch of cayenne pepper

¾ cup raisins

⅓ cup diced cilantro

Sea salt to taste

1. In a large, lidded saucepan, sauté onion, garlic, and cumin in a small amount of water over medium-high heat until onion is translucent, stirring frequently.

2. Add eggplant, peppers, carrot, turmeric, curry powder, and garam masala. Stir to mix for 1 minute, then add tomato, tomato paste, and vegetable broth. Cover and cook over medium heat for 20 minutes, stirring occasionally, until peppers and eggplant are soft.

3. Add cayenne, raisins, and cilantro. Simmer for another 5 minutes. Season with salt. ❋

*TIP:*
- *This dish is delicious served over couscous or rice.*

# NUTTY NOODLES WITH VEGETABLES

*Preparation time: 25 minutes*
*Cooking time: 25 minutes*
*Makes 4 servings*

1   onion, sliced
½   red pepper, seeded and diced
½   green pepper, seeded and diced
2   jalapeño peppers, seeded and diced
2   cups chopped broccoli
1   large carrot, cut in thin strips
¼   cup chopped fresh basil
2   tablespoons sesame seeds
1   pound whole wheat spaghetti or other pasta, cooked
½   cup low-fat chunky peanut butter
¼   cup light tamari or soy sauce
2   tablespoons rice vinegar
2   tablespoons minced fresh ginger
2   cloves garlic, minced
2   tablespoons sweetener (dry or wet)
3   green onions, sliced
1   cucumber, diced
    Sea salt to taste

1. Heat ¼ cup water over medium-high heat in a large saucepan. Add onions, peppers, broccoli, carrots, basil, and sesame seeds. Cover and cook for 5–10 minutes.
2. Remove cover and cook for an additional 5 minutes, until most of the water has evaporated. Stir in pasta. Set aside, but keep warm.
3. In separate saucepan, add peanut butter, tamari, rice vinegar, ginger, garlic, and sweetener. Cook over medium heat, stirring constantly, until mixture is smooth. Pour over noodles.
4. Top with green onions and cucumbers. ✳

*TIPS:*
- *Different vegetables can be added to or removed from this recipe. Snow peas and cauliflower are both great substitutes for broccoli.*
- *To make beautiful and easy julienne strips of carrot, use a vegetable peeler or julienne peeler.*
- *This is a great dish for kids.*

# PORTABELLAS WITH SPINACH AND RICE

*Preparation time: 25 minutes*
*Marinating time: 15 minutes–2 hours*
*Grilling or baking time: 15–25 minutes*
*Makes 4 servings*

4 large portabella mushrooms
4 tablespoons tamari
4 tablespoons balsamic vinegar
4 tablespoons red wine
4 cloves garlic, minced or pressed
2 cups cooked rice
8 cups fresh spinach, steamed until wilted, then drained

1. Clean the mushrooms and remove the stems.
2. Prepare the marinade by combining tamari, vinegar, wine and garlic in a large bowl. Whisk to blend.
3. Place the mushrooms upside down in the marinade and let stand for at least 10–15 minutes and up to 2 hours.
4. Remove mushrooms from marinade (reserve marinade). Place top-side up in a baking dish, cover, and bake for 25 minutes at 450° F. You can also grill these on an outdoor grill for 15 minutes.
4. Turn mushrooms over and pour reserved marinade into mushroom' cavities. Bake or grill until mushrooms can be pierced with a skewer, about 5 minutes longer.
5. Fill mushrooms with rice and spinach, and serve. ❋

*TIP:*
- *Many other vegetables are delicious baked as well. Zucchini, eggplant, sweet potatoes, peppers, and asparagus all make great accompaniments.*

# PUMPKIN GNOCCHI WITH
# ITALIAN VEGETABLE SAUCE

*Preparation time: 25 minutes*
*Cooking time: 25–30 minutes*
*Makes about 45 gnocchi*

| | |
|---|---|
| 1 | 15-ounce can pumpkin puree |
| 2¾ | cups whole wheat pastry flour |
| 1 | teaspoon sea salt |
| 1 | medium onion, sliced in long strips |
| 1 | vegetable bouillon cube |
| 1 | tablespoon oregano |
| 1 | 15-ounce can diced tomatoes |
| 4 | large zucchinis, sliced |

1. Mix pumpkin and flour to make a soft dough. If necessary, add more flour so dough holds together and is not sticky.
2. Divide dough into 4–5 sections and place on a floured surface. Roll each piece into a rope about 1 inch in diameter. Cut the rope into 1-inch pieces.
3. Boil a large pot of water with salt. Add gnocchi to the boiling water and cook until the gnocchi rises to the surface and floats, about 5 minutes. Depending on the size of your pot, you may need to cook them in batches. Remove from the water and set aside.
4. In a large saucepan over medium heat, sauté onion, bouillon, and oregano with ¼ cup water until onions are soft, about 5–10 minutes. Add tomatoes and zucchini. Cover and cook for 5–7minutes more, until zucchini is softened.
5. Put vegetables on top of gnocchi and serve immediately. ❋

*TIPS:*
- *When making the gnocchi, be careful not to overwork the dough. It's best to mix by hand rather than using a food processor. Do not use spelt flour in this recipe, because the gnocchi will dissolve in the water.*
- *This is a delicious and satisfying recipe that is surprisingly easy to make. The orange color of the gnocchi in contrast with the red and green of the vegetables is very appealing to the eye.*

# SCRUMPTIOUS BAKED VEGETABLES
# WITH FRESH SPINACH

*Preparation time: 45 minutes*
*Cooking time: 20 minutes if oven-roasting; 15 minutes if grilling*

DIET
VARIETY

1 medium onion cut into 1-inch chunks, layers separated
1 green bell pepper, seeded and cut into bite-sized pieces
1 sweet potato, cut into bite-sized pieces
1 head broccoli, cut into bite-sized pieces
½ pound button mushrooms, stems removed
1 pint cherry tomatoes
1 medium zucchini, cut into bite-sized pieces
  Garlic powder
  Onion powder
  Black pepper
8 cups fresh spinach

*For the sauce:*

2 tablespoons balsamic vinegar
2 tablespoons maple syrup
1 tablespoon sesame seeds
2 tablespoons freshly squeezed orange juice
1 teaspoon finely chopped ginger
1 teaspoon onion powder
1 clove garlic, minced

1. Prepare all vegetables except the spinach and place in a large baking pan lined with foil. Sprinkle with garlic powder, onion powder, and black pepper.
2. Preheat oven to 450° F and cook vegetables for 25 minutes.
3. While vegetables are cooking, whisk together all sauce ingredients in a medium-sized bowl.
4. Place spinach in a large serving bowl, add cooked vegetables, and mix in sauce. Serve immediately. ❈

*TIP:*
- *The vegetables can also be grilled. You can prepare them up to a day in advance for quick assembly later.*

# SOUTHWESTERN CALZONES

*Preparation time: 30 minutes*
*Rising time: 45–60 minutes*
*Cooking time: 25–30 minutes*
*Makes 8–10 calzones*

*For dough:*
- 2 **cups warm water**
- 2 **teaspoons brown sugar**
- 2 **teaspoons yeast**
- 4 **cups whole wheat flour**
- ½ **cup wheat gluten**
- ½ **teaspoon sea salt**

*For filling:*
- 2 **cups of your favorite salsa**
- 2 **cups corn**
- 1 **can black beans**
- ½ **cup vegan cheese**
- ¼ **cup green onions**
- ¾ **cup chopped black olives**

1. For the calzone dough, add the brown sugar to the water and stir to dissolve. Sprinkle the yeast in. Stir to dissolve. Set aside for 5 minutes to let the yeast bloom.
2. Meanwhile, combine flour, wheat gluten, and salt in a large bowl. Add the yeast mixture and stir with a wooden spoon until dough forms. Turn the dough out onto a clean, lightly floured surface and knead for about 10 minutes, or until the dough becomes smooth and elastic.
3. Cut the dough into eight equal pieces. Roll dough pieces into smooth balls and place them on a nonstick baking pan about 2 inches apart. Cover with plastic wrap and set in a warm, draft-free area to rise for 45 minutes to 1 hour.
4. Add all filling ingredients to a bowl and set aside.
5. Preheat oven to 425° F.
6. On a lightly floured surface, roll each dough ball out into a circle about 6–8 inches in diameter. Place 2–3 heaping tablespoons of filling in the center of the circle, wet the edges of the dough with a little water, and fold the sides together. Pinch the edges shut with your fingers or a fork.
7. Place calzones on a nonstick baking sheet and bake for 20–30 minutes, until tops are lightly browned.
8. Serve hot. ✻

*TIP:*
- *These calzones can be served with Quick Marinara Sauce (p. 107) or your favorite salsa.*

# SPAGHETTI SQUASH WITH SAVORY HERBS

*Preparation time: 25 minutes*
*Baking time: 45 minutes*
*Makes: 4 servings*

1 spaghetti squash
1 onion, diced
5 cloves garlic, pressed
1 vegetable bouillon cube
2 cups diced fresh tomatoes
1 tablespoon minced fresh parsley
1 tablespoon minced fresh basil
½ teaspoon minced fresh sage
½ teaspoon dried tarragon
  Sea salt and black pepper to taste

1. Preheat oven to 350° F.
2. Cut squash lengthwise and clean out seeds. Place squash cut sides down on a nonstick baking sheet. Bake for 45 minutes or until the squash is easily pierced with a sharp knife. Remove squash from oven and set aside to cool enough to be easily handled.
3. Sauté onion and garlic with a little water in a medium-sized skillet over medium heat until onion is soft. Add bouillon, tomatoes, parsley, basil, sage, and tarragon, and cook for 3–4 minutes. Season with salt and pepper. Set aside.
4. Using a fork, gently pull the strands of squash away from the peel. Place the strands into a large serving bowl.
5. Add sautéed vegetables to squash and mix gently until squash is covered. Serve warm. ❀

*TIPS:*

- *Spaghetti squash should be an even light yellow with no bruises. It can be stored at room temperature for up to 3 weeks and is available year-round, although its peak season is in the fall.*
- *Spaghetti squash is a dieter's dream! It has a high amount of fiber and very few calories.*

# TOMATILLO TORTILLA BAKE

*Preparation time: 15 minutes*
*Cooking time: 30 minutes*
*Makes 6 servings*

DIET
VARIETY

2   **bags baked tortilla chips, crumbled**
1   **26-ounce jar of salsa**
1   **15-ounce can corn**
1   **15-ounce can pinto beans, drained**
8   **tomatillos, husks removed, chopped**
¼ **cup water**
2   **jalapeño peppers**
½ **cup cilantro**
2   **cloves garlic, minced**
   **Sea salt to taste**
2   **avocados, chopped**

1. Preheat oven to 350° F.
2. Crumble baked tortilla chips into mixing bowl. Add salsa, corn, and beans. Mix well. Spread in the bottom of a 9 × 12 nonstick baking dish. Cover and bake for 30 minutes.
3. While baking, prepare tomatillo mixture. In small saucepan, add tomatillos, water, and peppers. Boil for about 15 minutes, until vegetables are soft. Pour into the bowl of a food processor and puree, adding cilantro, garlic, and salt to taste. Add additional water if a thinner sauce is desired. Set aside.
4. Remove tortilla bake from oven and let cool for 15 minutes. Serve drizzled with tomatillo sauce and topped with avocados. ❋

*TIP:*
- *This is an easy and simple dish, great for children to prepare.*

# VEGETABLE LASAGNA

*Preparation time: 30 minutes*
*Cooking time: 1 hour*
*Makes 9–12 servings*

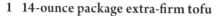

DIET
VARIETY

1 14-ounce package extra-firm tofu
5 cups fresh spinach
4 cloves garlic
1 tablespoon dried oregano
1 tablespoon dried basil
½ teaspoon sea salt
1 recipe Quick Marinara Sauce (p. 107) or 6 cups marinara sauce
1 10-oz package no-cook lasagna noodles

1. Preheat oven to 350° F.
2. Combine tofu, spinach, garlic, oregano, basil, and salt in food processor. Blend until smooth. Set aside.
3. Spread ½ cup marinara sauce over bottom of a 9 × 13 baking dish. Layer with noodles, then top with half the tofu mixture and ½–1 cup marinara sauce. Top with another layer of noodles, remaining tofu mixture, and another layer of marinara sauce. Finish with a third layer of noodles and remaining sauce.
4. Cover with foil and bake for 1 hour. Wait 10 minutes before serving. ❉

*TIP:*
• *You may want to add additional marinara sauce to this recipe if you like a juicier lasagna.*

# VEGETABLE POT-PIE STEW

*Preparation time: 25 minutes*
*Cooking time: 50 minutes*
*Makes 6 servings*

*For the stew:*
- 1 medium onion, chopped
- 2 cups cooked pinto beans
- 4 cups water
- 2 tablespoons Vegit brand seasoning or bouillon
- 1 teaspoon ground mustard
- ¾ cup peas
- ¾ cup chopped carrots
- ¾ cup diced potatoes

*For the dumplings:*
- 1½ cups whole wheat flour
- ¾ teaspoon baking soda
- Pinch sea salt
- ½ cup nondairy milk

1. Add onion to a large saucepan and sauté with a little water over medium-high heat until translucent.
2. Add beans, water, Vegit or bouillon, and mustard. Bring to a boil.
3. Add peas, carrots, and potatoes. Reduce heat to medium and simmer for 20 minutes, until vegetables are cooked through.
4. Meanwhile, mix flour, baking soda, and salt in a medium mixing bowl. Add milk and stir until dry ingredients are moistened.
5. Gently drop dough by rounded tablespoons into simmering stew. Cook uncovered over low heat for 10 minutes. Then cover and cook for 7–10 minutes more.
6. Serve immediately. ❀

*TIP:*
- *If you prefer, add additional vegetables.*

# ZESTY BULGUR STEW

*Preparation time: 10 minutes*
*Cooking time: 65 minutes*
*Makes 3 quarts*

DIET
VARIETY

1   15-ounce can chickpeas, drained and rinsed
½   cup bulgur
½   cup yellow lentils
6   cups water
1   tablespoon Vegit brand seasoning or 1 bouillon cube
1½ cups diced butternut squash
1   medium onion, diced
1   teaspoon cayenne pepper
1   teaspoon sea salt
1   tablespoon ground coriander

1. Place chickpeas, bulgur, lentils, water, and Vegit or bouillon in a soup pot. Bring to a boil, then simmer, partially covered, for 30 minutes.
2. Add the squash and continue to cook for 15 minutes.
3. Stir in the onion, cayenne, and salt. Cook 15 minutes more.
4. Add the coriander and simmer for 5 more minutes.
5. Serve immediately. ✽

*TIPS:*
  • *If a hotter dish is desired, add more cayenne pepper.*
  • *To save time, frozen butternut squash can be substituted for fresh.*
  • *This spicy dish is best served shortly after preparation.*

# ZUCCHINI CRABLESS CAKES

*Preparation time: 25 minutes*
*Cooking time: 30 minutes*
*Makes 12 cakes*

½ cup minced celery

½ cup chopped onion

½ cup grated carrot

2  medium zucchini, grated

½ small green or red bell pepper, minced

¼ cup chopped parsley

1  14-ounce package firm tofu, drained and crumbled

½ cup Green Garden Mayonnaise (p.50)

1  tablespoon Old Bay seasoning

2  teaspoons dry mustard

1  teaspoon sea salt

8  slices whole wheat bread, toasted and crumbled into bread crumbs
   (2 generous cups)

½ teaspoon paprika

1. Preheat oven to 350° F.
2. In large skillet over medium-high heat, add ½ cup water, celery, onion, carrot,
   zucchini, peppers, and parsley. Sauté until onion is translucent.
3. In a separate bowl, combine crumbled tofu, mayonnaise, Old Bay, dry mustard,
   and sea salt. Mix well.
4. Stir vegetables into tofu mixture. Add bread crumbs.
5. Shape into ½-inch thick patties and place on nonstick baking sheet. Sprinkle
   paprika on top of patties. Bake for 30 minutes.
6. Remove and let cool for 30–40 minutes before serving. ❀

*TIPS:*
- *You can serve these crabless cakes with horseradish if you like.*
- *These cakes also make delicious sandwiches.*

# SIDE DISHES

Basil Pepper Corn
Beets with Greens
Caribbean Moro
Carrot Bake
Cilantro Green Beans
Cranberry Applesauce
Creamed Cauliflower
Ethiopian Vegetables
Garlic Green Beans and Mushrooms
Lentils and Greens
Quick Butternut Squash
Seasoned Green Beans and Potatoes
Stewed Tomatoes
Tasty Potatoes and Kale
Twice-Baked Southwestern Potatoes
Zesty Succotash

# BASIL PEPPER CORN

*Preparation time: 20 minutes*
*Makes 6 servings*

1 medium onion, chopped
2 garlic cloves, minced
Sea salt and cayenne pepper to taste
4 ears raw corn, shaved (about 3–4 cups)
1 large or 2 small red peppers, seeded and diced
1 heaping tablespoon chopped fresh basil

1. Over medium heat, sauté onion and garlic with ¼ cup water in a large lidded skillet. When onions become soft, add a pinch of cayenne pepper and sea salt.
2. Add corn, red pepper, and basil. Cover and cook 3–5 minutes.
3. Season with more salt and cayenne pepper if needed. ❀

*TIPS:*
- *This can be served as a warm or cold dish.*
- *The flavor of red peppers is essential for this recipe. The sweetness of these peppers works better than the flavor of green peppers.*

# BEETS WITH GREENS

*Preparation time: 15 minutes*
*Cooking time: 20 minutes*
*Makes 6 servings*

4   medium beets
4   cups fresh greens (your choice)
1   tablespoon stone-ground or Dijon mustard
2   tablespoons lemon juice
2   teaspoons light soy sauce
1   tablespoon fresh dill (or 1 teaspoon dried dill)

1. Wash the beets and cut off the tops.
2. Peel the beets and slice them into ¼-inch-thick rounds. Steam over boiling water until tender, about 20 minutes.
3. In a separate pan, sauté greens in a small amount of water.
4. In a small bowl, mix mustard, lemon juice, soy sauce, and dill. Pour over greens and cook 2 minutes.
5. Add the beets. Serve hot. ✽

*TIPS:*
- *Beet tops are nutritious and tasty. Young leaves make a colorful addition to salads, and more mature leaves can be steamed for a delicious vegetable side dish.*
- *Check your local farmers' market for the wide variety of beets now being grown. Colors range from orange to red-and-white striped, and the flavors are subtly different.*

# CARIBBEAN MORO

*Preparation time: 10 minutes*
*Cooking time: 25 minutes*
*Makes 4 servings*

DIET
VARIETY

1   medium onion, diced
3   cloves garlic, minced
½   green pepper, diced
½   cup cilantro, chopped
2   vegetable bouillon cubes
2¼ cups water, separated
1   15-ounce can pigeon peas or pinto beans, drained and rinsed
3   rounded tablespoons tomato paste
1   cup rice

1. Combine onion, garlic, green pepper, cilantro, bouillon, and ¼ cup water in a medium (3-quart) saucepan over medium-high heat. Bring to a simmer and cook until onion and pepper are soft.
2. Add beans and tomato paste. Cook for two minutes. Add remaining water and rice.
3. Bring to a boil, then reduce heat to low and cover. Cook for 30–40 minutes, until water is absorbed and rice is tender. Serve. ❈

*TIPS:*
- *This dish is good served with diced avocados or shredded lettuce.*
- *Black beans can also be used in place of pigeon peas or pinto beans.*

# CARROT BAKE

*Preparation time: 15 minutes*
*Cooking time: 20 minutes*
*Makes 6 servings*

DIET
VARIETY

2    **pounds carrots, washed, peeled, and finely grated**
½    **cup reserved carrot-steaming liquid**
4    **tablespoons diced onion**
1½ **tablespoons horseradish**
½    **cup Green Garden Mayonnaise (p. 50)**
½    **teaspoon sea salt**
¼    **teaspoon black pepper**
1    **cup dry bread crumbs**

1. Preheat oven to 375° F.
2. In a large saucepan, bring 8 cups water to a boil. Add carrots and cook until tender, about 10 minutes. Drain; reserve ½ cup liquid.
3. Meanwhile, in a large mixing bowl, combine onion, horseradish, mayonnaise, salt, and pepper. Add carrots and reserved carrot liquid. Spread mixture in a 2-quart baking dish. Top with bread crumbs.
4. Bake for 20 minutes, until top of Carrot Bake is slightly crisp. ✽

# CILANTRO GREEN BEANS

*Preparation time: 20 minutes*
*Cooking time: 15 minutes*
*Makes 6 servings*

1  large onion, diced
½  green pepper, diced
2  vegetable bouillon cubes or 1 teaspoon low-sodium Vegit brand seasoning
2  teaspoons minced garlic
¼  cup chopped fresh cilantro
2  pounds green beans, diced

1. Over medium heat, sauté onions, green peppers, bouillon or Vegit, garlic, and cilantro in ¼ cup water until onion is translucent.
2. Add diced green beans, cover, and cook for 8–10 minutes, until beans soften. Serve hot. ❋

*TIPS:*

- *You can add other vegetables to this recipe, such as carrots and snow peas. When adding other vegetables, make sure you add additional cilantro, garlic, onions, peppers, and, if desired, Vegit or bouillon.*
- *This dish works well served over brown rice as an entrée.*
- *During the summer months, as I am harvesting the vegetables from my garden, I have found this recipe to work well with the older, more mature green beans that for one reason or the other were not harvested when they were first ready to be picked. The dicing and the cilantro make this a very delicious dish, so do not discard the tougher, older green beans; use them in this recipe.*

# CRANBERRY APPLESAUCE

*Cooking time: 20–25 minutes*
*Makes: 6 servings*

DIET
VARIETY

**1½ cups fresh cranberries**

**5   cups apples, peeled, cored, and diced**

**½   cup water**

**8   ounces unsweetened apple juice concentrate**

**1   teaspoon cinnamon**

1. Combine all ingredients in a covered saucepan. Cook over medium heat until cranberries and apples are soft.
2. Uncover for the last 5–10 minutes. If necessary, add additional water and/or sweetener.
3. Cool before serving. ❃

*TIPS:*
- *Use this delicious applesauce as a topping for pancakes or waffles.*
- *This recipe can be modified by adding 3 cups of seedless red grapes in place of apples and eliminating the cinnamon.*

# CREAMED CAULIFLOWER

*Preparation time: 20 minutes*
*Cooking time: 10 minutes*
*Makes 6 servings*

DIET
VARIETY

4   cups cauliflower florets
1   cup vegetable broth
¾   cup raw cashews
5   tablespoons vegan parmesan cheese (or nutritional yeast)
½   cup soy milk
3   tablespoons white miso
1   tablespoon Dijon mustard
    Freshly ground black pepper and sea salt to taste
½   cup white wine

1. Steam cauliflower over boiling water.
2. Meanwhile, place vegetable broth, cashews, parmesan cheese (or nutritional yeast), milk, miso, and mustard in the bowl of a food processor. Blend until smooth.
3. Pour mixture into a medium saucepan and bring to a boil. Reduce heat to low and cook, stirring constantly, until sauce thickens.
4. Add salt and pepper to taste. Stir in wine.
5. When cauliflower is cooked, remove from heat and place in a large serving bowl.
6. Pour sauce over cauliflower and serve immediately. ✽

*TIP:*
* *Other vegetables can be steamed and added to this recipe as well. Mushrooms, broccoli, and asparagus are good with this sauce.*

# ETHIOPIAN VEGETABLES

*Preparation time: 30 minutes*
*Cooking time: 30 minutes*
*Makes 6 servings*

2  large white potatoes, peeled and diced
2  cups green beans, cut into 1-inch sections
2  large carrots, peeled and sliced
2  cups corn
1  medium onion, finely chopped
2  cloves garlic, minced
2  serrano peppers, seeded and minced
1  teaspoon turmeric
1  teaspoon ground cumin
1  teaspoon curry powder
1  teaspoon sea salt
1  15-ounce can diced tomatoes
1  teaspoon fresh lime juice

1. Place potatoes in a covered medium-sized saucepan. Add water and bring to a boil. Cook for 12 minutes.
2. Add green beans, carrots, and corn. Cover and cook for 8 more minutes.
3. Drain the potatoes, carrots, green beans, and corn in a colander.
4. In large skillet, sauté onion, garlic, and serrano peppers with ½ cup water for about 4 minutes. Stir in the seasonings and sauté for 1 minute more.
5. Add boiled vegetables, diced tomatoes, and lime juice. Cook for 7 to 10 minutes over medium heat, stirring frequently.
6. Serve hot. ❈

*TIP:*
- *If possible, serve with ingera, Ethiopian flatbread. However, if this is not available, use warmed tortillas or brown rice.*

# GARLIC GREEN BEANS AND MUSHROOMS

*Preparation time: 20 minutes*
*Cooking time: 10–15 minutes*
*Makes 4 servings*

1 **pound green beans**
1 **pound mushrooms**
1 **teaspoon sesame seeds**
6 **cloves garlic, minced**
1 **jalapeño pepper, diced**
2 **tablespoons seasoned rice vinegar**
2 **tablespoons tamari**

1. Rinse the beans, trim the ends, and break into 1-inch pieces. Steam over boiling water until tender, 7 to 10 minutes.
2. Rinse and slice the mushrooms.
3. Heat ¼ cup water in a skillet over medium heat. Add sesame seeds, garlic, and jalapeño, and sauté for 3 minutes.
4. Stir in the vinegar and tamari. Add the mushrooms and cooked beans. Cook 5 minutes, then transfer to a serving dish. ❀

*TIPS:*

- *Fresh green beans should be smooth, soft, and velvety for best flavor and texture. Pass them by if they are wrinkled and leathery.*
- *The papery skins on garlic can be easily removed using a chef's knife. Lay the flat edge of the blade on top of the garlic clove and hit it firmly with the palm of your hand. You should hear a slight cracking sound as the skin breaks. Then it can be easily peeled from the clove.*
- *My mother likes green beans with tarragon. When adding tarragon to this recipe, do not add rice vinegar, tamari, sesame seeds, or jalapeño.*

# LENTILS AND GREENS

*Preparation time: 25 minutes*
*Cooking time: 15–20 minutes*
*Makes 8 servings*

1  large onion, sliced
1  teaspoon grated fresh ginger
2  tablespoons chopped fresh cilantro
3  cloves garlic, crushed
1  teaspoon ground cumin
½  teaspoon chili powder
2  cups lentils, cooked
2  pounds fresh Swiss chard
½  cup vegetable stock
   Sea salt and black pepper to taste
   Lemon juice to taste

1. In a medium saucepan, sauté onion, ginger, cilantro, and garlic in ¼ cup water over medium-high heat until the onion is translucent. Add the cumin and chili powder and cook for 1 more minute.
2. Add the lentils, Swiss chard, and vegetable stock. Reduce heat to low and cook for 7–10 minutes, stirring occasionally.
3. Season with salt, pepper, and lemon juice. ❋

*TIPS:*
- *Fresh Swiss chard is usually available year-round, but you can also use kale or collard greens.*
- *Canned pinto beans or red beans can be used to replace the lentils.*

# QUICK BUTTERNUT SQUASH

*Preparation time: 10 minutes*
*Cooking time: 15 minutes*
*Makes 4 servings*

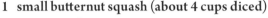

1  **small butternut squash (about 4 cups diced)**
½ **cup water (you may need to add ½ cup more)**
2  **teaspoons tamari or light soy sauce**
½ **teaspoon onion powder**
½ **teaspoon garlic powder**

1. Use a vegetable peeler to peel the squash. Then cut it in half and remove the seeds.
2. Cut the squash into 1-inch cubes (you should have about 4 cups). Place the cubed squash into a 5-quart pot with the water, tamari or soy sauce, onion powder, and garlic powder.
3. Cover and bring to an immediate boil, then reduce heat to medium and simmer until the squash is fork-tender, about 15 minutes. Serve warm. ❀

*TIPS:*
- *Try this recipe with other varieties of winter squash, such as delicata or kabocha. Each has its own distinctive flavor.*
- *Winter squashes are actually grown in the summer and ripen in the fall. Because they store well, many varieties are available year-round.*

# SEASONED GREEN BEANS AND POTATOES

*Preparation time: 8 minutes*
*Cooking time: 20 minutes*
*Makes 8 servings*

5  red potatoes
2  pounds fresh green beans
½ cup water
2  vegetable bouillon cubes
1  medium onion, diced
½ teaspoon Old Bay seasoning
3  teaspoons tamari or light soy sauce
   Sea salt and black pepper to taste

1. Scrub potatoes and cut into ½-inch cubes or wedges. Steam over boiling water until just tender when pierced with a fork. Rinse with cold water, drain, and set aside.
2. Rinse the green beans and remove the tough stems. Cut the beans into 1-inch sections.
3. In medium skillet, add green beans, water, bouillon, onion, Old Bay, and tamari or soy sauce. Cover and cook over medium-high heat, stirring occasionally, for 5–8 minutes.
4. Add cooked potatoes and season with salt and pepper. Continue cooking for about 5 minutes, using a spatula to turn the mixture gently as it cooks.
5. Serve immediately. ❀

*TIP:*
  • *Diced carrots can be substituted for potatoes.*

# STEWED TOMATOES

*Preparation time: 15 minutes*
*Makes 4 servings*

DIET
VARIETY

4   medium tomatoes, diced or blended
¼ cup onion, diced
¼ cup green pepper, diced
½ teaspoon sea salt
1   teaspoon Italian seasoning
¼ cup water
3   tablespoons whole wheat flour
½ cup nondairy milk
    Black pepper to taste

1. Dice or blend tomatoes and set aside.
2. Cook onion, peppers, salt, and Italian seasoning for 3 minutes in ¼ cup water.
3. Add tomatoes and continue cooking.
4. In a separate cup, mix flour and milk until lump-free. Add to tomato mix and stir until thick.
5. Add black pepper. ❋

*TIPS:*
• *This is good on top of your favorite toasted bread, potatoes, or biscuits.*

# TASTY POTATOES AND KALE

*Preparation time: 10 minutes*
*Cooking time: 30 minutes*
*Makes 6 servings*

4  red potatoes
1  bunch kale
1  onion, thinly sliced
1  carrot, finely grated
3  cloves garlic, minced
1  tablespoon fresh dill
2  teaspoons sesame seeds
2  tablespoons lemon juice
½  teaspoon black pepper
2  tablespoons tamari
1  tablespoon ground mustard

1. Scrub potatoes and cut into ½-inch cubes or wedges. Steam over boiling water until just tender when pierced with a fork. Rinse with cold water, drain, and set aside.
2. Rinse the kale and remove the tough stems. Cut or tear the leaves into small pieces. Heat ¼ cup water in large nonstick skillet and cook the kale. Set aside.
3. Heat ¼ cup water in a large nonstick skillet and add the onion, carrots, garlic, dill, and sesame seeds. Cook until onions are translucent.
4. Add cooked potatoes. Continue cooking until the potatoes begin to brown, about 5 minutes. Use a spatula to turn the mixture gently as it cooks. Add cooked kale.
5. In a small cup, mix lemon juice, black pepper, tamari, and mustard.
6. Add sauce to potato/kale mixture. Cover and cook, turning occasionally, for 2 minutes. ❈

*TIPS:*
- *Studies show that the calcium in kale is actually better absorbed and utilized by the body than the calcium in cows' milk.*
- *Collard greens, another excellent calcium source, substitute nicely for the kale in this recipe. However, you will need to briefly parboil the greens before adding them to this recipe.*
- *As always, if you don't have fresh dill, this can be replaced with dill seeds.*

# TWICE-BAKED SOUTHWESTERN POTATOES

*Preparation time: 20 minutes*
*Baking time: 1 hour 20 minutes*
*Makes 6 servings*

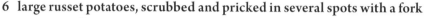
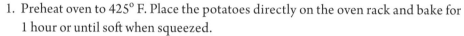

6 large russet potatoes, scrubbed and pricked in several spots with a fork
⅓ cup soy milk
½ teaspoon sea salt
½ teaspoon garlic powder
¼ teaspoon cayenne pepper
1 15-ounce can corn, drained
1 15-ounce can pinto beans, drained and rinsed
¼ cup chopped cilantro

1. Preheat oven to 425° F. Place the potatoes directly on the oven rack and bake for 1 hour or until soft when squeezed.
2. Remove potatoes from the oven, cut in half lengthwise, and let stand until easily handled but still warm.
3. Scoop out the potato pulp into a large bowl, leaving a ¼-inch-thick shell. Place the potato shells in an 8 × 12 casserole or baking dish.
4. With a potato masher, mash the pulp and add milk, salt, garlic powder, and cayenne. Fold in corn, pinto beans, and cilantro.
5. Spoon mixture back into potato shells. Bake for 20 minutes or until lightly browned. While potatoes are baking, make the salsa.

*Fresh tomato salsa:*
6 plum tomatoes, diced
1 small onion, diced
¼ cup chopped cilantro
¼ teaspoon garlic powder
2 tablespoons vinegar
Sea salt and black pepper to taste

1. Combine all ingredients.
2. Serve over potatoes. ❀

*TIPS:*
- *Additional vegetables can be added to these potatoes, such as grated carrots, chopped spinach, and/or chopped broccoli.*
- *You can also top the potatoes with a little soy cheese.*

# ZESTY SUCCOTASH

*Preparation time: 30 minutes*
*Makes 4 servings*

| | |
|---|---|
| 1 | small onion, finely chopped |
| ½ | large red pepper, seeded and diced |
| ½ | large green pepper, seeded and diced |
| 1½ | tablespoons jalapeño pepper, seeded and minced |
| 2 | cloves garlic, minced |
| 1½ | cups corn |
| 1½ | cups edamame, shelled |
| 3 | tablespoons red cooking wine |
| 2 | heaping tablespoons chopped fresh parsley |
| 1 | tablespoon chopped fresh basil |
| 1 | teaspoon dried oregano |
| ½ | teaspoon sea salt |

1. In a large skillet, sauté onion, peppers, and garlic with ¼ cup water over medium heat.
2. When onions become soft, add corn, edamame, and wine. Cook for 5–7 minutes, stirring constantly.
3. Stir in parsley, basil, oregano, and salt.
4. If needed, season with black pepper and serve at once. ❁

TIP:
- *Edamame can be purchased in the frozen food section of most grocery stores, often in the health food section. This soy bean has a wonderful nutty flavor and is being substituted here for traditional lima beans.*

# DESSERTS

Amazingly Delicious Date Fruit Pie
Apple Gingerbread Upside-Down Cake
Cheese(less) Cake with G-Mom's Nutty Pie Crust
Chocolate Banana Pie
Coconut Mango Pudding
Fresh Strawberry Pie
Frozen Banana Cream
Fruit Pudding
Mint Chocolate Pudding
Mixed Fruit Cobbler
No-Bake Peanut Butter Bars
No-Fat Cookies
Pineapple Cherry Cake
Quick Banana Loaf
Vegan Chocolate Cake
Vegan Pumpkin Pie

# AMAZINGLY DELICIOUS DATE FRUIT PIE

*Preparation time: 25 minutes*
*Makes 8 servings*

DIET
VARIETY

*Crust:*

1   cup pitted dates
1½ cups walnuts (or pecans)
1   teaspoon vanilla extract
½   cup shredded coconut
½   teaspoon cinnamon

*Topping:*

**Sliced fresh fruit (strawberries, blackberries, blueberries, raspberries, peaches, bananas, grapes, pineapple, mangoes, pomegranates, kiwis, etc.)**

1. Blend all crust ingredients in a food processor at high speed until a paste forms.
2. Press into a pie pan and chill until ready to add fruit.
3. Arrange fruit on top of pie.
4. Cool for 1 hour before serving. ❋

*TIP:*

- *This is delicious topped with a scoop of soy ice cream.*

# APPLE GINGERBREAD UPSIDE-DOWN CAKE

*Preparation time: 20 minutes*
*Cooking time: 35 minutes*
*Makes 9 servings*

DIET
VARIETY

3   medium Jonathan (or other tart) apples, peeled, cored, and sliced
2   tablespoons brown sugar
¾   cup whole wheat flour
¾   cup oat flour
1   teaspoon baking soda
¾   teaspoon baking powder
1   teaspoon ground cinnamon
2   teaspoons ground ginger
½   teaspoon allspice
½   cup unsweetened applesauce
⅔   cup molasses
2   egg replacers (4 teaspoons powdered Ener-G Egg Replacer
    and 6 tablespoons water)
1   teaspoon vanilla extract
¼   cup water

1.  Preheat oven to 350° F.
2.  Put apples in medium saucepan with a little water. Cover and cook 3–4 minutes over medium heat, until soft. Add brown sugar and stir to combine.
3.  In a small mixing bowl, combine flours, baking soda, baking powder, cinnamon, ginger, and allspice. Set aside.
4.  In a separate bowl, mix applesauce, molasses, egg replacers, vanilla, and water. Add to the dry ingredients and mix well.
5.  Spread softened apple–brown sugar mixture evenly on the bottom of a 9 × 9 baking dish. Pour batter over apples.
6.  Bake uncovered for about 35 minutes, or until a toothpick inserted in the center of the gingerbread comes out clean.
7.  While still warm, place a serving plate over cake pan and carefully turn the cake over so it comes out onto the plate. If necessary, push apple slices back into place. Serve warm. ❈

*TIP:*
*   *If desired, nondairy milk can be used in place of water.*

# CHEESE(LESS) CAKE WITH
# G-MOM'S NUTTY PIE CRUST

*Preparation time: 15 minutes*
*Chilling time: 2 hours*
*Makes 8 servings*

DIET
VARIETY

1   12-ounce box extra-firm silken tofu
¾   cup water
5   tablespoons dry sweetener
2   tablespoons cornstarch
2   tablespoons lemon juice
1   teaspoon lemon extract
1   teaspoon coconut extract
½   teaspoon vanilla extract
1   recipe G-Mom's Nutty Pie Crust (see following page)
    Fresh blueberries, sliced strawberries, and sliced kiwi, for topping

1. Crumble tofu into a saucepan. Add water and dry sweetener and bring to a boil.
   Add cornstarch, lemon juice, lemon extract, coconut extract, and vanilla extract.
   Reduce heat and simmer gently for 3 minutes.
2. Pour mixture into a blender or food processor and blend until very smooth.
3. Pour the mixture into prepared pie crust and smooth the top with a rubber spatula.
   Refrigerate until firm and cold, about 2 hours.
4. Spread fresh fruit evenly over the top before serving. ❋

*TIP:*
  • *Other fruit toppings can be used on this cheesecake. Fresh sliced peaches or cherry pie*
    *filling can be substituted for the fruit.*

# G-MOM'S NUTTY PIE CRUST

*Preparation time: 10 minutes*

1 cup ground nonfat or low-fat graham crackers
½ cup ground walnuts
½ cup coconut
7 tablespoons apple juice

DIET
VARIETY

1. Blend graham crackers and walnuts in a food processor. Transfer to a bowl and add coconut and apple juice. If mixture does not form into a ball, add 2–4 additional tablespoons of apple juice. Press into a 9-inch nonstick pie pan. ✳

TIP:
- *If you desire a cinnamon flavor, add 1 teaspoon of ground cinnamon.*

# CHOCOLATE BANANA PIE

*Preparation time: 15 minutes*
*Chilling time: 2 hours*
*Makes 8 servings*

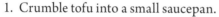

1   12-ounce box extra-firm silken tofu
½ cup cocoa powder
½ cup dry sweetener
¾ cup soy milk
1   teaspoon vanilla extract
2   tablespoons cornstarch mixed with 2 tablespoons sugar
2   medium bananas, sliced
¼ cup crushed nuts
1   recipe G-Mom's Nutty Pie Crust (p. 145)

1. Crumble tofu into a small saucepan.
2. Add cocoa, dry sweetener, and soy milk. Bring to a boil. Add vanilla and cornstarch mixture. Reduce heat and simmer gently for 3 minutes.
3. Pour mixture into a blender or food processor, and blend until smooth.
4. Layer sliced bananas on bottom of prepared pie crust. Pour mixture over bananas and smooth the top. Sprinkle with crushed nuts.
5. Refrigerate until firm and cold, about 2 hours. ✽

*TIP:*
 • *12 ounces of semisweet (dairy-free) dark chocolate chips can be used in place of cocoa, sweetener, and the sweetener-cornstarch mixture.*

# COCONUT MANGO PUDDING

*Preparation time: 5 minutes*
*Cooking time: 10 minutes*
*Chilling time: 2 hours*
*Makes 4 servings*

1   **15-ounce can unsweetened coconut milk**
1   **cup fresh mangoes, finely diced**
½   **cup dry sweetener**
¼   **cup cornstarch**
1   **cup soy milk**
1   **teaspoon vanilla extract**
    **Sliced strawberries, for serving**

1.  Pour coconut milk into a medium-sized saucepan. Add mangoes and cook over medium heat for 3–5 minutes. Add dry sweetener and cornstarch, stirring constantly until thickened.
2.  Add soy milk and vanilla. Continue to cook, stirring, until thickened.
3.  Pour into serving dishes and refrigerate until thickened.
4.  Garnish with fresh strawberries. ❀

*TIP:*
•  *This pudding is delicious served with your favorite vanilla wafer.*

# FRESH STRAWBERRY PIE

*Preparation time: 30 minutes*
*Chilling time: 2–3 hours*
*Makes 8 servings*

| | |
|---|---|
| 2 | cups crushed low-fat graham crackers |
| ½ | cup apple juice |
| 1½ | cups sliced fresh strawberries |
| ¾ | cup water |
| 1 | cup frozen (or fresh) whole strawberries |
| 4 | tablespoons cornstarch |
| ⅓ | cup dry sweetener |

1. Crush graham crackers and mix with apple juice. Press graham cracker mixture into a 9-inch pie pan.
2. Layer sliced strawberries on top of the graham cracker crust. Set aside.
3. In a medium saucepan, boil whole strawberries in water until they start to dissolve. Mix cornstarch and dry sweetener, and add to boiling strawberries. Boil over medium-low heat, stirring constantly, for 3–4 minutes, until mixture thickens.
4. Once mixture is thick, pour into pie dish over sliced strawberries.
5. Refrigerate 2–3 hours before serving. ✳

*TIP:*

- *Other fruits can be used in place of strawberries. Both blueberries and peaches work well in this recipe.*

# FROZEN BANANA CREAM

*Preparation time: 15 minutes*
*Makes 4 servings*

DIET
VARIETY

3   **tablespoons cocoa powder**
3   **tablespoons dry sweetener**
½   **cup soy milk**
4   **frozen bananas**
½   **cup nondairy milk**
½   **teaspoon vanilla extract (optional)**

1. Bring cocoa, sweetener, and milk to a boil in a small saucepan. Reduce heat and cook for 15 minutes while stirring constantly. Remove from heat and set aside.
2. In the bowl of a food processor, blend bananas, milk, and vanilla until smooth.
3. Portion banana mixture into four serving bowls. Drizzle chocolate sauce on top of banana cream and serve immediately. ❋

*TIP:*
- *Fresh fruit can be used in place of chocolate topping.*

# FRUIT PUDDING

*Preparation time: 15 minutes*
*Cooking time: 20 minutes*
*Chilling time: 1 hour*
*Makes 9 servings*

4  cups mixed fruit (any combination of blackberries, raspberries, strawberries, pears, apples, or blueberries)

½  cup brown sugar

1  teaspoon cinnamon

½  cup apple juice or cranberry juice, separated

1  loaf of your favorite sweet bread (Lemon Poppy Bread, p. 26, or Quick No-Fat Cranberry Bread, p. 27)
   Vanilla soy ice cream, for serving

1. Preheat oven to 350° F.
2. Place the fruit in a large saucepan and add sugar, cinnamon, and ⅓ cup apple juice. Simmer over low heat for 5–10 minutes. Remove from heat.
3. Line bottom of 9 × 9 nonstick baking dish and sides of dish with slices of bread. Make sure there are no gaps between slices.
4. Pour fruit mixture into baking dish. Cover top of fruit mixture with extra-thin slices of bread. Drizzle with remaining apple juice and press down into fruit mixture. Cover and bake for 15 minutes.
5. Chill in the refrigerator for 1 hour before serving. Serve with a scoop of vanilla soy ice cream. ❋

# MINT CHOCOLATE PUDDING

*Preparation time: 6–7 minutes*
*Cooking time: 10 minutes*
*Chilling time: 2 hours*
*Makes 4 servings*

DIET
VARIETY

1½ cups soy milk
⅓ cup maple syrup
¼ cup cocoa powder
3 tablespoons cornstarch
½ teaspoon mint extract

1. Whisk milk, maple syrup, cocoa powder, and cornstarch together in a medium saucepan. Cook over medium heat, stirring constantly, until pudding is thickened.
2. Stir in mint extract and pour into individual serving dishes.
3. Cool in refrigerator for 2 hours before serving. ❅

*TIPS:*
- *Recipes using cocoa powder will tend to be much lower in fat than those using baker's chocolate.*
- *This dessert can be garnished with toasted almonds or fresh fruit or berries.*

# MIXED FRUIT COBBLER

*Preparation time: 10 minutes*
*Baking time: 25 minutes*
*Makes 6 servings*

6   cups berries; if frozen, thaw first (use blueberries, blackberries, raspberries, or a mixture)
3   tablespoons whole wheat pastry flour
½   cup dry sweetener

1   cup whole wheat pastry flour
2   tablespoons dry sweetener
1½  teaspoons baking powder
½   cup nonfat soy milk or rice milk

1. Preheat oven to 400° F.
2. In a large mixing bowl, combine berries, 3 tablespoons flour, and ½ cup sweetener. Spread in a 9 × 9 baking dish.
3. Combine 1 cup flour, 2 tablespoons sweetener, and baking powder in a separate bowl. Mix with a fork or your fingers until the mixture resembles coarse corn meal. Add the soymilk or rice milk and stir to mix.
4. Spread the mixture over the berries (don't worry if they're not completely covered) and bake until golden brown, about 25 minutes. Let cool for 10 minutes before serving. ❋

*TIPS:*
- *Most baking powder is made with aluminum. Look for aluminum-free baking powder in your natural foods store.*
- *Other sweeteners that may be substituted to sweeten the berries are ¼ cup rice syrup, maple syrup, honey, or strawberry all-fruit spread. To reduce the sugar in the topping, try substituting 2 tablespoons date paste for the sugar.*

# NO-BAKE PEANUT BUTTER BARS

*Preparation time: 15 minutes*
*Chilling time: 1 hour*
*Makes 9 servings*

8   ounces low-fat graham crackers, crushed
¼   cup crushed walnuts
½   cup shredded, unsweetened coconut
⅓   cup powdered sugar
⅓   cup peanut butter
⅓   cup nondairy milk
1   cup chocolate chips
5   tablespoons rice milk

1. Crush graham crackers and walnuts in food processor. Remove and pour into a medium-size bowl. Mix in coconut, powdered sugar, and peanut butter.
2. Slowly add milk and mix. If mixture does not hold together, continue adding additional milk until all ingredients stick together. Don't be afraid to use your hands.
3. Spread mixture evenly into a 9 × 9 nonstick baking dish.
4. In a saucepan, melt chocolate chips together with rice milk over medium heat. Stir until smooth.
5. Spread chocolate mixture on top of peanut butter mixture. Refrigerate for 1 hour or until hardened. Cut into squares and enjoy! ❅

*TIPS:*
- *These make a great holiday treat.*
- *These bars are rich, creamy, sweet, and satisfying—everything a dessert should be!*

# NO-FAT COOKIES

*Preparation time: 15 minutes*
*Chilling time: 30 minutes*
*Makes 2 dozen cookies*

1   banana, mashed
½ cup nondairy milk
½ cup brown sugar
1   cup oat flour
1   cup whole wheat flour
1   teaspoon baking soda
½ cup oatmeal
½ cup applesauce
3   tablespoons maple syrup
⅓ cup shredded coconut
⅓ cup chopped walnuts
½ cup raisins

1. Preheat oven to 350° F.
2. Mix banana, milk, and brown sugar in a small bowl.
3. In separate bowl, mix flours, baking soda, and oatmeal.
4. Add banana, brown sugar, and milk to dry ingredients. Then add applesauce, maple syrup, coconut, walnuts, and raisins. Mix until dry ingredients are moistened.
5. Drop by tablespoon-sized amounts onto prepared baking sheet.
6. Bake for 12 minutes. Let cool; place cookies in a container and cover. ❋

*TIP:*
- *This recipe is also good with chocolate chips or peanut butter chips.*

# PINEAPPLE CHERRY CAKE

*Preparation time: 10 minutes*
*Baking time: 25–30 minutes*
*Makes 9 servings*

DIET
VARIETY

1   15-ounce can crushed pineapple (not drained)
1   16-ounce can sour cherries (or 2⅓ cups fresh cherries,
    or 1 15-ounce can light cherry pie filling)
½   cup flaked coconut
1   cup wheat flour
1   cup rolled oats
1   teaspoon baking powder
⅓   cup brown sugar
1½ cups apple juice

1. Preheat oven to 400° F.
2. Mix pineapple, cherries, and coconut, and spread in a 9 × 9 baking dish.
3. In a separate bowl, combine flour, oats, baking powder, and brown sugar. Spread this mixture evenly on top of fruit.
4. Pour apple juice evenly on top of dry mixture in baking dish.
5. Bake 25–30 minutes. ❁

*TIPS:*
- *You can use fruit that is fresh, frozen, or canned. Frozen berries can be used straight from the package.*
- *To save time, you can use a dry cake mix in place of the flour, oats, baking powder, and sugar. Try to find a cake mix that is low in sodium and fat.*
- *This is a quick and easy recipe.*

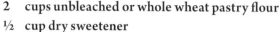
# QUICK BANANA LOAF

*Preparation time: 10 minutes*
*Cooking time: 50 minutes*
*Makes 9 servings*

| | |
|---|---|
| 2 | cups unbleached or whole wheat pastry flour |
| ½ | cup dry sweetener |
| ½ | teaspoon cinnamon |
| 1½ | teaspoons baking soda |
| 4 | ripe bananas |
| ¼ | cup water |
| 1 | teaspoon vanilla extract |
| ½ | cup chopped walnuts |
| ½ | cup chocolate chips (optional) |

1. Preheat oven to 350° F.
2. Combine the flour, dry sweetener, cinnamon, and baking soda in a mixing bowl.
3. In a larger, separate bowl, mash the bananas, and stir in water and vanilla. Mix thoroughly. Add the flour mixture, walnuts, and chocolate chips. Mix to combine.
4. Spread into 9 × 9 nonstick baking pan and bake for 45–50 minutes, until a toothpick inserted into the center comes out clean. ❋

*TIPS:*
- *Raisins can also be added to this recipe.*
- *Whole wheat pastry flour is ground from a softer variety of wheat than all-purpose whole wheat flour and makes lighter, finer-textured baked goods, while retaining the bran, germ, and other nutrient-rich parts of the whole wheat berry. Look for whole wheat pastry flour in the baking section of natural foods stores.*

# VEGAN CHOCOLATE CAKE

*Preparation time: 10 minutes*
*Cooking time: 30 minutes*
*Makes 9 servings*

*For the cake:*

2   cups flour (unbleached or whole wheat pastry flour)
1½  teaspoons baking soda
1½  teaspoons baking powder
¾   cup dry sweetener
½   cup cocoa
1   ripe banana, mashed
½   cup applesauce
2   egg replacers (4 teaspoons powdered Ener-G Egg Replacer
    and 6 tablespoons water)
¾   cup water
¾   cup soy milk
1   teaspoon vanilla extract

*For the frosting:*

2¾  cup powdered sugar
4   rounded tablespoons cocoa powder
7   tablespoons water
1   teaspoon vanilla extract
    Chopped walnuts (optional)
    Grated coconut (optional)

1. Preheat oven to 350° F.
2. Mix flour, soda, baking powder, dry sweetener, and cocoa in a large mixing bowl.
3. In a separate bowl, mash banana and stir in applesauce, egg replacers, water, milk, and vanilla. Mix thoroughly. Add to the flour mixture and mix well.
4. Spread into a 9-inch nonstick baking pan and bake for 30 minutes, until a toothpick inserted into the center comes out clean.
5. While cake is cooling, mix powdered sugar, cocoa powder, water, and vanilla. Spread evenly on top of cake. Top with walnuts or coconut, if you choose. ❋

*TIP:*

- *Ener-G Egg Replacer product can be purchased in the health food section of most grocery stores. Follow the package directions to make the equivalent of 1 egg.*

# VEGAN PUMPKIN PIE

*Preparation time: 10 minutes*
*Baking time: 40 minutes*
*Makes 8 servings*

DIET
VARIETY

2  cups cooked mashed pumpkin
1  12.3-ounce box silken tofu
½  cup dry sweetener
1  teaspoon cinnamon
¼  teaspoon nutmeg
¼  teaspoon ginger
1  recipe G-Mom's Nutty Pie Crust (p. 145)

1. Preheat oven to 350° F.
2. Put the pumpkin in a food processor with tofu, dry sweetener, cinnamon, nutmeg, and ginger. Process until very smooth.
3. Pour the mixture into the crust. Bake for 40–45 minutes or until the filling is set and the crust is golden. Let pie cool to room temperature before serving. ❀

# RECIPE INDEX